Sharpening the Legal Mind

SHARPENING THE LEGAL MIND

How to Think Like a Lawyer

WILLIAM POWERS JR.

EDITED BY JOHN DEIGH

UNIVERSITY OF TEXAS PRESS *Austin*

Printed in the United States of America
First edition, 2023

♾ The paper used in this book meets the minimum requirements of ANSI/NISO Z39.48-1992 (R1997) (Permanence of Paper).

LIBRARY OF CONGRESS CATALOGING-IN-PUBLICATION DATA

Names: Powers, William, Jr., 1946–2019, author. | Deigh, John, editor.
Title: Sharpening the legal mind : how to think like a lawyer / William Powers ; edited by John Deigh.
Description: First edition. | Austin : University of Texas Press, 2023. | Includes bibliographical references and index.
Identifiers: LCCN 2022010525 (print) | LCCN 2022010526 (ebook)
ISBN 978-1-4773-2641-1 (hardcover)
ISBN 978-1-4773-2642-8 (pdf)
ISBN 978-1-4773-2643-5 (epub)
Subjects: LCSH: Law—United States—Methodology—History. | Jurisprudence—United States—History. | Law—Study and teaching—United States—History.
Classification: LCC KF380 .P69 2023 (print) | LCC KF380 (ebook) | DDC 349.73/09—dc23/eng/20220831
LC record available at https://lccn.loc.gov/2022010525
LC ebook record available at https://lccn.loc.gov/2022010526
doi:10.7560/326411

Contents

Editor's Preface

Bill Powers loved teaching. He taught at the University of Texas at Austin for more than forty years, including even during the years he was serving as the dean of the law school and president of the university. He took special interest and joy in introducing beginning students to a new world of ideas and new ways of thinking. This book is an expression of that interest and joy. How lawyers understand and reason about the law can appear deeply mysterious to people outside the legal profession. The mystery of legal thought is particularly daunting for first-year law students as they embark on their legal careers. Powers's exposition demystifies the law. His aim is to explain, starting from inside the profession and then moving to the higher reaches of academic legal thought, how lawyers think about law and what approaches teachers of law take to imparting to their students the ideas and methods of legal analysis.

His general subject is jurisprudence, a field of study that encompasses questions about the nature of law and legal systems, the reasoning of judges in deciding cases, and the relation of law to justice and morality generally. He treats this subject topically at first and then, beginning with chapter 5, expounds a rich history of the development of legal thought in the United States from the American Revolution to the present. His discussion in the later chapters illuminates both the different approaches to the interpretation of law that have emerged throughout the history of American jurisprudence and the social forces that gave rise to problems of law and new schools of interpretation that developed in response to them. Both readers unfamiliar with studies in jurisprudence and specialists will find much to learn from the account of law in these pages.

Powers had a distinguished career at UT, as a professor in the law school, as the school's dean for five years, and as the university's twenty-eighth president. He served in that last office from 2006 to 2015. His tenure was longer than that of any of his predecessors but one, and it was notable for the extensive restructuring of the undergraduate education he oversaw, the founding of a medical school he initiated, and his steadfast defense of the university and the academic values at its core from efforts by politically powerful outsiders to shrink and distort its research mission. After stepping down as president, Powers resumed full-time teaching in the law school, and jurisprudence was one of the classes he most enjoyed teaching. His interest in the subject stretched back to the early 1970s when he was a law student at Harvard University and the managing editor of the *Harvard Law Review.* Jurisprudence at Harvard in those days was dominated by the legal process school, a homegrown movement that the most influential scholars and teachers on the law faculty had founded in the 1950s, and all of Harvard's top law students became steeped in its methods and ideas. But, in addition to his immersion in the methods and ideas of the legal process school, he studied moral and political philosophy with John Rawls, whose eminence in those fields was unsurpassed and whose great work, *A Theory of Justice,* had just been published. Powers's earliest publications, after he graduated from law school in 1972, were on central questions of jurisprudence, and he continued to write on these questions in his later work.

Powers, at the time of his death in March 2019, had completed a draft of this book. His estate had entrusted the book manuscript to the University of Texas School of Law, and Ward Farnsworth, the school's dean, asked me to prepare a final draft for publication. The manuscript had already undergone a review by the University of Texas Press, and the reports from the two external readers from whom the Press had solicited evaluations were favorable. It was, however, an unfinished manuscript. It read, as one of the readers observed, more like a second draft. This reader suggested several revisions, and on reading the entire manuscript, I saw that even further revision would be necessary. While the early chapters were polished, the later ones were rougher and, in a sense, thinner. The exposition lacked coherence in several places, and accounts of the ideas and theories of major thinkers in the history of Western philosophy, which are integral to the book's central argument, needed correction and enrichment to accomplish their purpose. There were also, scattered throughout, errors of fact and quotation. The reader had identified some of these in his report. But others were less easily ferreted out and had ramifications within the text that complicated the changes that were needed to correct them. On the whole, then, it seemed to me that extensive rewriting to remove these problems and errors was preferable to an excessive reverence for the text that I had inherited.

The chapters to which I made the most extensive revisions are chapters 4 and 7. A substantial part of chapter 4 is a history of legal positivism from its appearance in ancient Greek thought to its major twentieth-century statements in the works of Hans Kelsen and H. L. A. Hart. Powers followed the once, and perhaps still, popular view that Thomas Hobbes's theory of law is the first statement of legal positivism in the modern era. Hobbes's theory, however, is not a version of legal positivism, despite its superficial similarity to the theory expounded by the great nineteenth-century jurist John Austin, which was the standard statement of positivism prior to Kelsen's and Hart's. Rather it falls within the modern natural law tradition as that tradition emerged from the work of Hugo Grotius. Legal positivism in the modern era originates in the work of Jeremy Bentham, particularly his attack on the natural law theory embedded in Blackstone's *Commentaries.* Accordingly, I replaced Powers's discussion of Hobbes as the founder of modern positivism with a corresponding discussion of Bentham, and because Austin was Bentham's disciple, I revised Powers's discussion of Austin to bring out the commonalities between their two versions of the theory.

Chapter 7 covers the two dominant schools of moral philosophy in the modern era: utilitarianism and the version of natural law theory that originates with Grotius. In his treatment of the latter, Powers focused on the moral and political theories of Jean-Jacques Rousseau, Immanuel Kant, and John Rawls. The works of Rousseau and Kant from which he drew in expounding their theories are difficult to interpret and not easily explained to readers who have little or no acquaintance with them. Both philosophers invented special vocabularies in which they stated their theories, and this technical terminology heightens the demands on the reader's understanding of their texts. Keeping to the thrust and core of Powers's expositions, I rewrote them in large part to make them more faithful to these works and to convey more clearly the ideas of their authors that Powers was presenting. For the same reasons but to a much lesser extent, I also made changes to his exposition of Rawls's theory.

In the final chapter, Powers draws lessons about the various methods lawyers use to think about the law and argues for understanding the law's indeterminacy in light of those methods. He intended to illustrate this understanding of the law's indeterminacy in a paragraph near the end of the chapter discussing a civil case, *Ghassemieh v. Schafer,* and the problem it is commonly used to represent in a first-year torts course. But after writing the paragraph's topic sentence and starting a new sentence with a mention of the case, he abruptly stopped, leaving the paragraph to be completed later. I have supplied an analysis of the problem in this case that I believe Powers had in mind, but I cannot be certain of whether the analysis I give matches how he saw the case as representing this problem or whether he would have endorsed my analysis as an illustration of his thesis that there is no one correct method that lawyers should use to interpret the law in a given case. Unfortunately, he left no notes that could shed light on these uncertainties. My analysis, then, should be taken as offered in the spirit of the approach to interpreting the law for which Powers argued in this final chapter.

Powers had left out almost all of the citations he intended to give in the first seven chapters. They were to be added later. He inserted footnote numbers for these but, with very few exceptions, left the footnotes blank. Chapters 8 and 9 did not even have footnote numbers, though they did contain plenty of material for which citations needed to be provided. With the help of Laura Moedano, who had been Powers's research assistant, I have filled in all but a few of the missing citations and added citations to material in need of them in chapters 8 and 9 as well as to material I added in revising the manuscript. Moedano's help in this regard and in editing the main text was indispensable, and I incorporated many of the suggestions she made for improvements to the prose. I am very grateful for all the work she put into the project, as I am sure Powers was for the work she did for him. I also owe thanks to Mitch Berman, who read and commented on the entire manuscript. I sought his advice when I first took on the project, and the suggestions he made then and later were most helpful. David Rabban gave me valuable feedback on chapter 5, and Ward Farnsworth gave me excellent advice on drafting this preface. I am thankful, too, for the help of Sarah Shamburg. Her handling of the organizational matters that went with the project was invaluable.

Bill Powers's death was a great loss to Texas Law and the university. It is an honor for me to be able to contribute to preserving his legacy through the publication of this book—his last and most significant contribution to the field of jurisprudence.

—JOHN DEIGH

Sharpening the Legal Mind

ONE

"I WANT MY OLD MIND BACK"

THE FIRST YEAR OF LAW SCHOOL is designed in large part to teach students to "think like lawyers." The nominal content of usual first-year courses—torts, contracts, property, civil procedure, and constitutional law—is not unimportant, but lurking beneath the surface is a more basic, if amorphous, goal. We try to give students a set of analytical skills that constitute "legal" reasoning. Implicit in all of this is an underlying assumption that lawyers have access to a special way of thinking that gives them a shared methodology for solving legal problems.

The first year of law school is famously difficult and frustrating, as we see in the autobiography *One L* and the film adaptation of the novel *The Paper Chase*. There are many reasons for this. One reason is that the Socratic method insists that students actively solve problems in front of their peers, rather than merely sit back and absorb information. When Christopher Columbus Langdell introduced the case method to the Harvard Law School in the late nineteenth century, he was motivated primarily by a desire to develop and inculcate a more scientific method of legal reasoning.[1] Today, the idea is that the Socratic method helps students learn to think. It should not be surprising that a teaching method that demands daily participation from students causes performance anxiety even when it is done "gently." Most first-year law students are adults who have done little other than attend school and who have not yet resolved major questions about their lives.[2] And for the first time in their lives, many students receive what they think are mediocre grades.

But there are deeper reasons. Learning to think like a lawyer requires a certain intellectual posture toward the world—a posture that privileges reason, conceptualism, and formalism—that can evoke strong emotional and intellectual reactions. Consider the following exchange:

> Professor: Is there a contract here?
> Student: I think it's unfair to make the consumer pay.
> Professor: But that wasn't my question. Is there a contract?

Lurking beneath this seemingly simple (and typical) exchange is a complex and controversial view of the world. Implicit in the professor's "legal" posture are the underlying assumptions, to name only two, (1) that law and morals (fairness) are and should be distinct and (2) that human problems can and should be resolved with reference to a limited set of criteria (designated as being relevant by the appropriate legal rules) rather than with reference to the totality of circumstances. We will return later to the complexity of this seemingly simple exchange and its implicit underlying assumptions. For now, it is sufficient to suggest that the intellectual posture this exchange demands of students can be deeply troubling. Putting aside the student's reaction to the *result* in the particular case, it should not be surprising that an attempt to reorient the student's *way of thinking* about human problems might be met with resistance.

It is sometimes said that legal education sharpens the mind by narrowing it.[3] When the *Paper Chase*'s indomitable Professor Kingsfield tells his students that although they came to him with minds full of mush, they will leave thinking like lawyers, he invokes the goal of sharpening their minds. The author of a cartoon in a law school newspaper understood the other side of the coin:[4]

The point is not that learning to think like a lawyer is pernicious. To the contrary, we shall see in due course that learning to think like a lawyer has many desirable consequences, *including* sharpening one's mind. My point is that learning to think like a lawyer can be a double-edged sword that raises serious issues about how we should think about and interact with the world and with other people. Teaching students to think like lawyers is often done without explicit attention to what is at stake, sometimes leaving students with a vague but unexamined feeling that someone is messing with their minds.

Teaching students to think like lawyers can be a source of frustration in yet another way. Law students often accuse their teachers of "hiding the ball," by which they usually mean the teacher asks a lot of questions without providing many answers. Athenians made the same complaint about Socrates. It is an annoying trait. Students focus on the surface of things, such as the professor in the earlier exchange declining to tell the students whether there really was a contract. In response to this complaint, students are usually told that the "answer" to a specific doctrinal question is less important than their ability to develop and rely on their own analytical skills. The important hidden ball is not the one on the surface, however.

It is the one hidden at a deeper level, the one containing the appropriate ground rules of analysis. Why is it that certain types of argument—let us say careful attention to facts, or to language, or to a result's economic consequences—receive nods of approval from a teacher, whereas other types of argument—let us say answers that refer to broad conceptual rules or to the student's moral or religious beliefs—receive scowls or flippant rebuffs? However explicit a teacher might be about providing guidance on *doctrinal matters,* explicit instruction or even discussion about the underlying *ground rules* of analysis—that is, about what it means to think like a lawyer—is rarer.

Ground rules seem to change from class to class. In one class, the teacher demands exquisite and precise knowledge of the facts underlying a dispute or careful attention to the words of a statute and scorns reference to broad "first principles" or concepts. In another class, it is just the opposite. In still another, the social desirability of a specific result is the focus of attention. In some classes economic theory seems to be the universal solvent; in others it is political theory, history, or a certain theory of literary interpretation. Pity the poor student who must learn to think like a lawyer on such shifting sands.

In fact, for all of the talk about teaching students to think like lawyers, there is widespread disagreement about what thinking like a lawyer actually means. There is even doubt among some law teachers that there is *anything* special about legal reasoning. For them, the idea of thinking like a lawyer is a mere façade.

Curricular choices and pedagogical styles reflect this disagreement. What counts as a good answer in any given class—not just in result but in style of reasoning—depends heavily on the professor's underlying (often implicit) assumptions about legal reasoning. When students complain that they do not know what a particular professor is looking for, they often are wiser than they know. Different professors *are* looking for different things—in terms of styles of argument—because they have different (sometimes implicit) jurisprudential assumptions about what it means to think like a lawyer. Some think that legal reasoning is conceptual, formal, and distinct from morals or politics. Others think that legal analysis cannot meaningfully be distinguished from politics or morals. Some professors think that legal interpretation is like literary interpretation; others do not. It is not surprising, then, that their choices of relevant material and appropriate argumentation will vary dramatically. Not surprising, that is, except to students who are not privy to the jurisprudential disagreements.

Not every professor has a self-conscious, coherent theory of legal reasoning. Most have eclectic teaching styles that reflect complex views about what it means to think like a lawyer. Nevertheless, American legal education reflects various jurisprudential schools of thought that have influenced different professors in various ways. Some teachers are strong adherents to a single school, but most rely selectively on various models of legal reasoning. But the fact remains that various schools of thought have influenced our views about what it means to think like a lawyer, and these views affect how we teach our students. It is not surprising that students find learning difficult when jurisprudential diversity lurks unannounced beneath the surface of their instruction.

THE IDEA THAT LAWYERS have a special way of thinking is important beyond the confines of law school classrooms. It is intimately tied to the idea of the rule of law. Put simply, the rule of law assumes that "impartial" judges decide cases by following "external" general rules and that "like cases are treated alike." As John Rawls puts it, the rule of law requires "the regular and impartial administration of public rules."[5] As such, it is "closely related to liberty,"[6] because it enables citizens to ascertain their legal obligations and act accordingly. Only if we have at least some shared criteria for ascertaining solutions to legal problems can we decide whether we are, in fact, ruled by "laws" and not by "men."

No serious, current student of American law thinks that the political values of individuals who occupy official legal positions make *no* difference to the outcome of legal disputes.

But unless lawyers share *some* common methods and criteria for solving legal disputes, the rule of law is nothing more than a façade. In fact, we shall see that doubt about whether lawyers have a special, viable method of solving legal disputes leads some people to argue that the rule of law *is* nothing more than façade.

It is not surprising that the confirmation process for nominees to the United States Supreme Court focuses on candidates' professed methods of legal reasoning. Nor is it surprising that, to the extent we might question our shared commitment to a common form of legal reasoning, we focus on candidates' political views. Part of the debate is about the extent to which, if at all, lawyers have access to a special, shared way of thinking. To what extent are they "following" the law instead of "creating" it? A first-year student's frustration about learning to think like a lawyer is a microcosm of a debate about the rule of law as a basis for social interaction. Both phenomena reflect struggles within and among competing jurisprudential camps.

JURISPRUDENCE IS, AMONG other things, an examination of what it means to think like a lawyer. Do lawyers, in fact, have a special method for solving legal problems, or does their claim to a special methodology mask the imposition of raw political power? If lawyers do have a special way of thinking, what are their underlying ground rules, assumptions, and implicit values? As a "philosophy of law," jurisprudence is akin to a philosophy of science, mathematics, music, or history. Just as philosophies of these disciplines attempt to understand and critique the underlying ground rules, assumptions, and implicit values of the discipline, jurisprudence attempts to systematize and critique the underlying ground rules, assumptions, and implicit values of legal reasoning.

In the first instance, jurisprudence involves an analysis of the *structure* of legal reasoning, not the *substantive content* of particular laws. Law's content raises interesting questions of social and political philosophy, such as the moral status of affirmative action, abortion, the market, the death penalty, and so on. In fact, much of the heat in law school classrooms is caused by heartfelt differences about issues such as these. But aside from the content of law, the very structure of law and legal reasoning has a profound effect on the way we view the world. It is this structure, not law's content, that is the primary focus of jurisprudence.

This does not mean that the structure of legal reasoning is not itself value-laden or related to law's content. In fact, we shall see that a defining feature for one prominent school of thought is a claim that the *form* of legal reasoning cannot be divorced entirely from the *substantive content* of our legal norms.[7] Nevertheless, the starting point of jurisprudence is the structure of legal reasoning, not the content of its rules.

AS A PHILOSOPHY OF "law" and of "legal" reasoning, the discipline of jurisprudence already contains a significant amount of content. Why should we investigate "legal" reasoning and develop a philosophy of "law" rather than, for example, "criminal law" reasoning to develop a philosophy of "criminal law"? Conversely, why not have a philosophy of social organization, of which law is merely a part? Of course, we do have such disciplines, which merely recognizes that the world can usefully be sliced in different ways. But the particular slice made by jurisprudence is useful only if "law" and "legal" reasoning are both sufficiently *discrete* and *integral* categories. One implicit claim of jurisprudence (and "law" school) is that legal reasoning is sufficiently distinct from other forms of reasoning so that we can profit from developing a special theory (and school) to understand it. Another implicit claim is that legal reasoning is sufficiently integral—that is, it transcends law's component parts—so that we can profitably group the component parts together.

This problem is not unique to law. We can study human life by focusing on molecules, cells, organs, individual human beings, families, or social organizations, to name a few of the possibilities. None of these focal points are intrinsically correct. Useful disciplines have grown up around each of them.

Similarly, we can profitably study legal disputes by focusing on individual cases, on doctrinal areas such as tort law or constitutional law, on groups of doctrinal areas such as private law or public law, or, even more generally, on social organization, of which law is simply a component part. In fact, the law school curriculum reflects a conclusion that various doctrinal areas, such as contract law, tort law, and so on, are sufficiently distinct from each other and homogenous within themselves that they should form distinct courses. Even within a doctrinal area such as tort law, further divisions can profitably be made between intentional torts, negligence, and so on.

What, then, makes a taxonomy that focuses on "legal" reasoning a useful one? We can take some comfort from the fact that *law* schools have grown up as distinct and integral departments within universities and that lawyers form their own "profession." Of course, this may be for reasons other than the nature of legal reasoning. Sociological and economic factors might help account for it. But they are some indication that thinking like a lawyer is both *sufficiently* different from other forms of thinking and *sufficiently* homogenous within itself to be a fruitful general category for study. Another indication is that, in political discourse, we extol the rule of "law," not the rule of "contracts" or the rule of "social norms." Lawyers, whatever their field, have access to a special way of reasoning that gives them a shared methodology for solving legal problems, and this methodology is, to some extent, different from the methodology of other disciplines.

In the end, it is likely that we can support some version of the claim that "legal reasoning" is a distinct but integral category. But for now it is important that we not merely assume it or overstate it. Thus, we should be open to differences in the reasoning processes of various areas of the law. For example, we should not rule out a priori the possibility that reasoning in constitutional law is different from reasoning in tort law. (In fact, some current jurisprudential theories suffer from an attempt to construct general theories of legal reasoning by focusing on the great constitutional issues of our time, without devoting enough attention to mundane, garden-variety issues of private law.)[8] Conversely, we should not assume a priori that legal reasoning is entirely distinct from reasoning in other normative disciplines, such as ethics, economics, history, literary criticism, political theory, and so on. Doing so would foreclose potentially fruitful analogies to these other disciplines. The issue here is the extent to which law is a homogeneous, autonomous discipline with its own ground rules, rather than merely a collection of separate disciplines or merely derivative of some other discipline. Indeed, the relationship between law and morals is itself one of the great issues in jurisprudence.[9] Its answer is something we need to think about, not something we can merely take for granted.

So although teaching students to think like lawyers seems to be a natural goal in an institution with the mission of educating prospective lawyers, we should not take for granted that legal reasoning is a homogeneous entity that cuts across various divisions within law itself or is necessarily distinct from reasoning in other disciplines. In the end, we can support a claim that *some* aspects of thinking like a lawyer transcend doctrinal divisions and *some* aspects of legal reasoning are different from reasoning in other disciplines, but these claims need to be investigated, not merely assumed. In short, we should not let the structure of jurisprudence as a discipline answer the very questions jurisprudence is designed to investigate.

WHAT, THEN, ARE the features of legal reasoning we should investigate to determine whether thinking like a lawyer is special and, if so, what its contours are? What are the ground rules for "correct" legal reasoning? What counts as a "valid" legal argument, and where do we get the criteria for making that determination? Are the criteria conventional, or are they grounded outside the practice of legal reasoning? What axioms or underlying assumptions, taken for granted but not themselves examined, seem to support legal reasoning? What are the underlying assumptions that legal reasoning makes about human nature, about our social structure, and about social institutions such as families or markets? What normative values seem to be implicit in legal reasoning? Perhaps most important, are there coherent theories that make various answers to these questions hang together in an elegant way? For example, do certain criteria of validity in legal arguments resonate with certain underlying assumptions about human nature and commitments to certain normative values? As we shall see, particular schools of jurisprudential thought have grown up around certain *sets* of answers to these questions that seem to cohere in a particularly satisfying way. It is these schools of thought, not merely answers to individual questions, that have had a powerful influence on our conception of what it means to think like a lawyer and, consequently, on legal education. And on our conception of the rule of law.

WE CAN APPROACH JURISPRUDENCE from either of two perspectives: We can start outside and work our way in, or we can start inside and work our way out. For the first approach, we might imagine a philosopher confronting law and analyzing it. Her inclination is to examine social or intellectual phenomena. Her skill is unpacking and understanding their intellectual structures. Some jurisprudential writing takes this perspective. Scholars whose basic academic discipline is ethics, analytical philosophy, political science, or sociology might use the analytical tools of their disciplines to study law from their own perspective.[10] This approach has the advantage of bringing a fresh eye to law, untainted by myopic familiarity. It is better able to escape capture by the very discipline it seeks to analyze. At the same time, there is a danger that a nonlawyer will examine a caricature of law without understanding fully the rich detail of legal reasoning as it would be understood by someone within the system.

For the second approach, which goes from inside to out, we might imagine a lawyer who participates in the practice of legal reasoning and encounters intellectual problems that prompt further inquiry. Reflecting on these problems, the lawyer might try to step outside the practice to gain a better perspective on the structure of the practice itself. Some jurisprudential writing takes this perspective.[11] It comes from within law schools, from scholars who, though they may use other disciplines to study law, are quite familiar with the practices of lawyering. The danger of this perspective is that the person studying law might unconsciously be captured by the very assumptions and reasoning processes he is attempting to study, but he is much less likely to construct a caricature of the practice he purports to analyze.

Either approach faces an obstacle of finding an "Archimedian point"[12] that is both sufficiently close to law to understand it and sufficiently divorced from law to gain critical perspective. My own approach will be to approach an Archimedian point, to the extent one can be approached at all, from inside of law, working outward. That is, we will begin with a practical legal problem that a lawyer or, more to the point, a first-year law student might confront, and then we will ask the kinds of reflective questions that a thoughtful practitioner of legal reasoning might ask. An inside/out approach is not intrinsically better, but it is the approach that more closely replicates the kinds of questions that confront law students in their first year.

From either starting point, however, an attempt to construct an Archimedian point can be treacherous. When we stand outside law to cast a cold eye back on its structure, where is it that we stand? We can step onto the ground of other disciplines, such as ethics, economics, history, or political theory, and use their tools to analyze legal reasoning, but then we are dependent on the soundness of those analytical tools. There is a temptation in this type of inquiry to search for truly firm ground, for a foundational discipline that can be used to study them all. There is a temptation to follow Plato out of the cave to see things as they "really" are.[13] Following the lesson of most twentieth-century philosophy, I will not try to find purely neutral, firm ground from which law can be justified or grounded. Nor will I try to establish a hierarchy of disciplines whereby some are more "basic" than others. We might never fully escape our own conventions of reasoning to understand or analyze them fully. All we can do is use our own conventions of reasoning to analyze themselves, which has obvious problems of circularity.

It may be possible, however, to gain some distance from *particular* conventions to get a better look at them. We can step from one discipline to another in order to gain some perspective and understanding of what it means to think like a lawyer—much as Monet's various paintings of the cathedral at Rouen can give us a better understanding of it—even though none is more "correct" than another.[14] Jurisprudence may not be able to validate one particular theory of legal reasoning as correct or to ground legal reasoning in uncontroversial assumptions. But we might gain a better understanding of what it means to think like a lawyer by looking at it from a variety of perspectives.

TO UNDERSTAND WHAT it means to think like a lawyer—or to understand more about the rule of law—we need to return to some "classical" issues that serve as a foundation for current jurisprudential debates but that have fallen out of fashion. Most current academic writing is technical and, understandably, written for experts. It usually assumes (sometimes implicitly) an understanding of previous debates that spawned current issues. Most law students (and some of their teachers) are not familiar with these historical debates. An understanding of the intellectual history of contemporary jurisprudential debates helps identify schools of thought that still have influence in legal education and helps place current issues in perspective. For example, legal education's infatuation with literary theory, economic theory, and political theory can profitably be seen partially as an extension of and response to jurisprudential debates of the previous generation of scholars. Even where current jurisprudential debates have gone beyond some of the basic problems that were resolved by previous generations, the problems themselves remain basic to legal reasoning, and they confront each generation of law students anew. So we will examine some of this intellectual history.

We may not be able to resolve all of the issues about what it means to think like a lawyer, but students who understand more about the debate can be better consumers of legal education. They can better understand the curricular and pedagogical disputes that surround them. They can gain insight into their relationship to law and to the aspects of legal reasoning that, on the surface, seem to bother them. At a minimum, they can understand their jurisprudential heritage.

In this sense, this book can serve as a "finishing school" that helps law students (and their teachers and other lawyers) understand the culture in which they work. It can also help citizens interested in the rule of law—and interested in what it means to ask whether judges are "following" the law or "making" the law—to understand some of the context and back stories that surround these issues. Then they can make up their own minds. These groups are my intended audience.

TWO

"THE CASE OF THE SPELUNCEAN EXPLORERS"

WE TEACH STUDENTS to think like lawyers primarily by having them read and analyze written opinions of appellate court judges. This is not because the style of reasoning contained in these opinions is the only (or even primary) mental activity practicing lawyers use. In fact, lawyers spend most of their time engaged in quite different intellectual tasks, such as negotiating contracts, drafting documents, investigating and analyzing empirical facts, making business decisions about their law offices, cross-examining witnesses, and so on. Much worthwhile reform in legal education—such as the growth of legal clinics—focuses on some of these other lawyering skills. "Learning to think like a lawyer" refers to a *special* task that lawyers perform in ascertaining their clients' "legal" obligations. Appellate opinions are models of judges engaged in that task. They are models of taking authoritative legal materials—such as statutes, contracts, or earlier judicial opinions—and using them to obtain an answer to what the law requires in a specific set of circumstances.

In a common law system, appellate opinions are themselves also important *sources* of legal obligations—especially in first-year subjects such as property, torts, and contracts. But they are a centerpiece of legal education, especially in the first year, mainly because they also provide models of the intellectual activity of ascertaining what the law "means." This is the specific intellectual activity to which the idea of thinking like a lawyer refers.

Appellate opinions are not the only models of legal reasoning about what the law means or requires. Law review articles and internal law firm memoranda might also serve as models. But appellate opinions are both authoritative sources of law *and* models of legal reasoning, so they serve double duty in the law school curriculum. And they are available.

Appellate court opinions might also serve as authority to resolve disputes about legal reasoning itself. Courts have authority to resolve substantial legal disputes, so why not also give them authority to create "law" on issues of legal reasoning? In fact, some courts occasionally purport to do this when they announce rules of statutory or contract interpretation. By and large, however, important disputes about the nature of legal reasoning are not expressly resolved by courts, leaving judges, lawyers, and scholars free to carry on their own "extralegal" debate about what it means to think like a lawyer.[1]

At any rate, judicial opinions are readily available models, and under current practice they serve as a law student's principal window into legal reasoning. Thus, they serve as a point of entry for examining the kinds of questions law students face when they are learning to think like lawyers, and so we begin by turning to such an opinion—albeit a fictional one. It appears in Lon Fuller's article "The Case of the Speluncean Explorers."[2]

LON FULLER SPENT MOST of his career in the middle of the twentieth century at Harvard Law School as one of the preeminent American legal philosophers of his generation. We will return to his work throughout this book. The depth of Fuller's thought is often camouflaged by the simplicity of his style. "The Case of the Speluncean Explorers" is straightforward and easy to read, but it raises deep questions. We will use it as a window to these questions, but it is worth reading in its entirety.

The article consists of fictional opinions written in the year 4300 by five justices of the Supreme Court of Newgarth. The case is an appeal from a conviction and death sentence of four spelunkers who killed and ate one of their company after being trapped in a cave for twenty-three days. They had carefully ascertained from doctors on the surface that they would not survive without sustenance. They agreed among themselves to select the victim by casting a die, although the victim reneged before the die was cast for him. The four defendants were convicted and sentenced under a statute that provided: "Whoever shall willfully take the life of another shall be punished by death."[3] Although the facts are unusual, the arguments contained in the justices' opinions are familiar examples of the main, competing styles of legal reasoning.

Chief Justice Truepenny, whose opinion serves mainly to lay out the facts, argues for affirming the conviction by simply quoting the statute and stating that it "permits of no exception applicable to this case, however our sympathies may incline us to make allowance for the tragic situation in which these men found themselves."[4] He argued the Court should join the jury and the trial judge in recommending that the Chief Executive grant clemency, which Truepenny was quite sure the Chief Executive would do.

Justice Keen voted to affirm the conviction. He first identified two issues that were not his job to decide: (1) whether the explorers were morally justified in killing their colleague, and (2) whether the Chief Executive should grant clemency (though Justice Keen did state that, were he the Chief Executive, he would do so). His role as a judge was solely to determine whether the defendants' conduct was proscribed by the statute. It was self-evident to him that, according to the "natural" meaning of the words, the defendants did "willfully take the life of another."[5] The only source of difficulty for the other justices, he said, was that they did not like the outcome. But that was irrelevant to their jobs. They should have distinguished between the *legal* aspects of the case, which are a judge's only appropriate concern, and its *moral* aspects, which are not.

Justice Handy voted to reverse the conviction, chastising his colleagues for obscuring a simple human problem with a "curtain of legalisms" and "tortured ratiocinations."[6] The real question is what the government of Newgarth should do with the defendants, which is a question of "practical wisdom" and "human realities," not "abstract theory."[7] Government is a "human affair" that should not be ruled by "words on paper or by abstract theories."[8] We should treat legal forms and abstract concepts not as ends in themselves but as instruments that are accommodated to the facts of the case at hand. Otherwise, law becomes inflexible and divorced from public sentiment, and it cannot long endure. The fact that 90 percent of the public thinks the defendants should not be put to death ought to be determinative. Depending on the clemency power of the Chief Executive is not sufficient, because a relative of Handy has informed him that the Chief Executive—who is a man of "stiff notions"—will not pardon the defendants.

For Handy, Truepenny's and Keen's scrupulous adherence to form is selective. While they think it is essential to orderly government that *judges* follow the letter of the law, they are quite willing to have other governmental officials—such as the prosecutor and the Chief Executive—exercise nearly unfettered discretion. Society would be better served if judges, too, exercise common sense based on the "realities" of a case.

Justice Foster relied on two independent grounds to reverse the conviction. First, he argued that the "positive" law of Newgarth did not extend to the cave. Positive law "is predicated on the possibility of men's coexistence in society,"[9] but this was not possible in the cave. Absent positive law, the explorers were in a "state of nature."[10] They did not violate Newgarth law because consent of the governed is the contractual basis of law generally, and their own agreement to cast a die created a law of its own. Their conduct was not so extraordinary. Every decision to build a highway or tunnel creates a risk of death. Even the decision to rescue the explorers here caused ten workmen to be killed when they were removing rocks from the opening of the cave. Why, then, was it not proper for the explorers to kill one of their group to save four?

Second, Foster argued that even if Newgarth law governed the explorers, they had not violated it. He professed subservience to the legislature, but the meaning of a statute is found in its *purpose,* not merely in its words. The Court had previously carved out an exception for self-defense, even though the words of the statute did not refer to such an exception, because the statute's purpose—to deter killing—would not be served by refusing to recognize self-defense. Similarly, enforcing the letter of the statute here would not deter a killing because "we may be sure that their decision whether to live or die will not be controlled by the contents our criminal code."[11] The legislature would not want courts to follow statutes literally to defeat the legislature's purpose any more than a parent would want a maid to "drop everything and come running" if she were, unbeknownst to the parent, in the act of rescuing the baby.

Justice Tatting, who was both sympathetic to the plight of the explorers and disgusted by their "monstrous act," was not convinced by either of Foster's arguments. First, how could the explorers not be governed by the "positive" law of Newgarth? Did this occur when they became trapped, or did this occur when they became hungry? If one of the explorers had attained the age of majority while in the cave, would the event have no effect on his "positive law" rights in Newgarth? In any event, the *Court* was bound by the positive law of Newgarth, even if the explorers were not. And Justice Foster's interpretation of "the law of nature" was topsy-turvy indeed, as it made the law of contracts more fundamental than the law of murder.

Second, Tatting argued that Justice Foster's invocation of the deterrent purpose of the statute was not helpful. Deterrence is just *one* purpose of the statute; another is an orderly outlet for retributive justice. Even if deterrence was the only purpose, could we say that the stigma of being labeled murderers and being executed would not have caused the explorers at least to wait a few more days? The standard rationale for the self-defense exception was not, as Foster argued, that deterrence was the statute's purpose. Instead, the self-defense exception rested on a conclusion that killing in self-defense was not "willful." If the criminal law should not be applied to reach results inconsistent with the goal of deterrence, how would Foster explain *Commonwealth v. Valjean,* where hunger was not allowed to excuse stealing a loaf of bread. In short, it is impossible to identify any "coherent and rational principle" underlying the law, making Justice Foster's reliance on such a principle fatally flawed. Not being able to adopt Justice Foster's methodology, and not being able to invent one of his own, Tatting withdrew from the case.

Justice Keen also attacked Justice Foster's methodology. Although Foster claimed to observe the time-honored principle of legislative supremacy, his method of identifying a "gap" in the statute and then resolving it in accordance with the statute's purpose actually permits him to rewrite statutes. His method of assigning a single purpose to a statute, as Tatting demonstrated, overlooks the fact that statutes have *multiple* purposes. To the contrary and more to the point, they have no real purpose at all. A statute against murder reflects a basic revulsion to murder; any attempt to give it more discrete purposes is like "the attorney who argued that a statute licensing physicians was a good thing because it would lead to lower life insurance rates by lifting the level of general health. There is such a thing as overexplaining the obvious."[12] Maybe the historic authors of the murder statute were actually worried about or repelled by anthropophagy.[13] We can never really know their original intent. If we cannot identify a statute's real purpose, how can we fill a "gap"? Foster's method reminded Keen of "the man who ate a pair of shoes. Asked how he liked them, he replied that the part he liked best were the holes."[14]

At the same time, Keen could not explain the exception for self-defense. He merely argued that the case at hand did not involve self-defense, so the purpose of this exception was irrelevant. Strict adherence to statutes would remind citizens that they are responsible for making law; if this had been done with the problem of self-defense, the legislature surely would have revised the statute.

So, with Tatting's decision to withdraw from the case, the Court was evenly divided, which meant that the lower court's conviction was left in place.

Fuller's own rendition of these opinions is much richer than these sketches, but even the sketches highlight the principal styles of argument we find in judicial opinions. As Fuller himself put it in a short postscript:[15]

> The case was constructed for the sole purpose of bringing into common focus certain divergent philosophies of law and government. These philosophies presented men with live questions of choice in the days of Plato and Aristotle. Perhaps they will continue to do so when our era has had its say about them. If there is any element of prediction in the case, it does not go beyond a suggestion that the questions involved are among the permanent problems of the human race.

BY FACING A SIMPLE, practical (albeit fictional) problem—deciding whether to affirm a conviction—the justices faced complex theoretical issues about legal reasoning. Deciding on a correct *result* required a decision about the proper *method* for resolving legal disputes. In fact, the point of disagreement among the various justices is almost entirely methodological. The justices do not seem to have significant disagreement about the facts. They do disagree about what facts are relevant, but this is itself a dispute about method, not about the facts themselves. The justices might disagree about the death penalty and anthropophagy, but if we take their arguments at face value, their principal source of disagreement is the appropriate role and method of judges. How, then, do the various justices differ?

ONE PLACE THE JUSTICES do not differ is in their common assertion that their job is to "follow" the law. They may differ about the proper method of ascertaining what the law means, but none of them saw himself as "disobeying" the law.

We often take for granted that judges should "follow" the law, but this is itself an important jurisprudential point. We might imagine a "legal" system in which officials who resolve disputes simply apply their own moral lights, much as a kaid who dispenses justice in a tribe. Our legal system, however, asks judges as well as other officials and individuals to defer to the authority of centrally promulgated "legal" norms. The fact that we take this aspect of legal reasoning for granted does not detract from its importance. Significantly, no justice in "The Case of the Speluncean Explorers" denied this requirement. We might suspect that each justice—most notably Handy but the other justices as well—was clever enough to reach a result they otherwise preferred notwithstanding the "legal" norms, but that is a question about the power and weakness of various methods of legal reasoning. On the surface, each justice nominally deferred to law. Even Handy purported to interpret law in light of *public* opinion, not his own moral values. The question was what the law required, and that depended on the appropriate method of legal reasoning.

Had the justices seen their role as determining the "morally correct" treatment of the explorers—had they openly seen themselves as "legislators"—they would have been required to articulate and debate the moral question of how the explorers deserved to be treated. Law school classrooms often focus on issues such as this—for example, whether a particular rule of tort law or contract law is socially desirable. These debates often make for lively discussion, especially if the topic itself is controversial. But they often take the posture of occurring "outside" of law, offering a critique of it, not inside of law, providing an interpretation of it.

This point is itself controversial. Handy, for example, would treat many factors—such as public opinion—as occurring inside law, whereas Keen would argue that they are outside. In fact, we shall see later that some jurisprudential schools assert that the inside/outside distinction is itself indefensible. A common source of confusion for students is uncertainty about whether a certain type of classroom discussion actually is occurring inside or outside of law. But classroom discussions often take the posture of being *openly* outside of the law, offering a critique of it, and these justices might have engaged in that kind of debate.

Some of the most heated debates about what the law *ought* to require are beside the point in regard to what the law *does* require. Including such debates in law school classrooms must rest either on the jurisprudential claim that they are actually inside of law or on the pedagogical claim that, although they occur outside of law, they are useful for lawyers to entertain. But the point here is that there is *another* source of disagreement about legal results and that this source of disagreement also leads to heated (jurisprudential) debate: What method should judges (and lawyers) use to ascertain what the law *does* require, putting aside our disagreements about what the law *should* require (and again leaving open the possibility for a *jurisprudential* conclusion that this distinction is itself unsound)? As before, at least on the surface of their opinions, it is on the issue of what method judges should use that the justices in "The Case of the Speluncean Explorers" disagreed.

How, then, do these justices disagree about method? They disagree on at least five important points: (1) What is the source of law? (2) How "formal" should formal law be? (3) How does law relate to morals? (4) What is the institutional relationship between courts and other institutions? and (5) How should we glean meaning from legal materials? The justices do not just disagree about these issues independently; each justice has views on individual issues that affect their answers to other issues. It is these *clusters* of answers that represent competing jurisprudential schools of thought, which in turn have influenced what it means to think like a lawyer and the concept of the rule of law.

FOR KEEN, THE *SOURCE* OF LAW is the official pronouncement of the legislature. Keen presumably would also recognize common law court decisions or constitutional provisions as sources of law because they are an exercise of authority by an official governmental body. For Keen, law is not found in nature, culture, or social goals; it is found in the pronouncements of official bodies that have authority in our system of government.

Keen's *method* of applying law is highly formal. A formal decision is one in which the decision maker, here the judge, uses less than all available relevant information by following a rule. The rule blocks out any information not invoked by a rule.[16] Thus, for Keen the only facts relevant to a legal decision were those identified by the statute: whether the explorers "willfully killed another human being." This was not because Keen thought other information might not be relevant to what the explorers deserved morally or what decision would be best for society. Maybe the explorers were decent folk whose execution would cause widespread sadness. Maybe the explorers were on the brink of curing cancer. Those facts might be relevant to ultimate questions of right, wrong, and social policy, but they were not identified by the statute. The statute served as an opaque screen by which the judge was precluded from considering them.

Formality is not the same as arbitrariness. A rule *maker* can (and presumably does) consider all relevant facts and policies when determining the content of a rule so that it produces generally desirable results. But formality demands that, once a rule is promulgated, it, rather than its generative policies, provides the ground for decision. The rule is opaque. It precludes the judge from looking through it to the underlying policies that generated it or to any other facts it does not expressly identify. We need to put to one side for the moment whether this type of decision-making is desirable or even possible. Those are questions we will need to examine later. The point is that this is what formality *purports* to do.

Keen also insists on rigorously separating law and morals. This does not mean that the content of legal norms does not often coincide with the content of moral norms. Indeed, one hopes that the law *makers* consult morality (or some normative system) when they enact laws. Nothing in Keen's insistence on the separation of law and morals suggests, for example, that morality, unlike law, does not proscribe murder. But a judge can and should *ascertain* what a law means independent of moral inquiry. If it turns out that law and morals conflict, so be it. That may be reason for lawmakers to *change* the law, but it does not affect a judge's interpretation of what a law *is*.

As we shall see, Keen's insistence on the rigorous separation of law and morals is the hallmark of a jurisprudential school called "positivism." Foster alluded to it when he distinguished between "positive" law and "natural" law. The former is found in the pronouncements of authoritative governmental bodies, whereas the latter is found in nature, independent of governmental action, and is closely associated with morals. Foster's own methodology of ascertaining what "positive" law means did not require a rigorous separation of law and morals, but he nevertheless reflected the influence of positivism by making this distinction. Keen is a staunch advocate of positivism.

Keen also had a particular view of the institutional role of courts and of their relationship to other governmental institutions. Courts should be absolutely subservient to legislatures. They should be passive, not active. They should defer to the will of the legislature (when the legislature has spoken) rather than independently shape the direction of the law. Few issues of contemporary jurisprudence have captured the attention of the American public as has the debate about judicial activism. Keen represents one side of this debate. With respect to legislatures, Keen's insistence on a passive role for courts resonates with a commitment to democracy. It also reflects underlying views about the relative competence and expertise of courts and legislatures. Legislatures are better equipped to gather information and gauge the public mood. In any event, Keen's jurisprudential position reflects an underlying assumption about values and about how the political world does and should work.

Judicial activism is not just an issue vis-à-vis legislatures. A judge must also decide whether courts should be active or passive vis-à-vis other institutions, such as executive branch decisions, private decisions about personal lifestyles, private decisions reflected in market transactions, and earlier decisions of a court itself. As we shall see, some courts have claimed to be passive toward some institutions, such as legislatures, but active toward others, such as private contracts reflecting market decisions. Keen was not faced with the court's posture toward these other institutions, and his principal reason for judicial subservience to the legislature—democracy—is not applicable to those institutions. So we cannot be sure what he would say.

Closely related to Keen's insistence that courts should be subservient to the legislature is an underlying belief that different governmental institutions play different roles in our social organization, and consequently, their methods of carrying out their tasks are different as well. The legislature's role is to *make* law; the court's role is to *interpret* it, at least when the legislature has spoken. Keen might find room for court-made common law on subjects the legislature has left open to judicial development. We just don't know.

Truepenny—whose opinion adds little to Keen's—also differentiated between the functions of the legislature and the executive branch. The Chief Executive's job is to grant clemency based on a methodology very different from the court's. That was not the court's job.

Finally, Keen relied on a theory of *interpretation* or of *meaning*. For Keen, the meaning of a statute can and should be gleaned from the *words* alone: Did the explorers "willfully" "kill" "another human being"? The self-defense exception was based on what it means to do something "willfully," not on the statute's overarching purpose or goal to promote a specific social policy. Keen's method was literalism. On the surface, literalism is different from formalism. Literalism is a view about meaning; formalism is a view about applying that meaning come hell or high water. At a deeper level, however, formalism and literalism are connected, as are most of Keen's judgments on individual jurisprudential points. We shall return to that connection in a moment.

KEEN'S JURISPRUDENCE IS defined by his individual beliefs in (1) positivism, (2) formalism, (3) a separation of law and morals, (4) subservience of courts to legislatures, and (5) literalism. If each of these issues were independent, we could imagine dozens of jurisprudential camps, but these issues are not entirely independent. Keen's position on one of them is related to his position on others. In this sense, his jurisprudence "hangs together" in a particularly elegant way.

Keen's commitment to formalism is related to his belief that courts are subservient to legislatures. A judge is supposed to consider what the legislature thinks is important, not what his own views on the subject, all things considered, indicate is a correct result. It is for the legislature, not the judge, to determine whether certain mitigating circumstances forgive what would otherwise be a "willful killing." If judges are to defer authority to legislatures, legislatures need a way to communicate their authoritative decision to the judges. Simple efficiency dictates that the legislature cannot itself meet to consider the facts of each case and make individual decisions, and it would be too unwieldy (indeed impossible) to dictate a rule in advance that considers every conceivable fact pattern. General rules, which refer to certain *salient* facts (and therefore are by their very nature formal) allow a legislature to promulgate norms that govern a wide range of cases.

A legislature could simply grant "real" authority to courts themselves by delegating authority or by promulgating standards that grant broad discretion, such as a "rule" that a person who *unreasonably* kills another human being will be given an *appropriate* punishment. But a legislature might not trust judges to make the right decisions and therefore try to control judges by promulgating a more formal rule. Formality is a way of containing the scope of a decision maker's considerations, thereby limiting her flexibility. This increases the likelihood that the decision maker will be "loyal."

We can see why a legislature might promulgate formal rules. But why would a *judge* adopt a formal methodology for applying those rules? The two issues are not identical, but they are closely connected. If a judge could consider facts, policies, and values not triggered by the rule itself, the judge would be less constrained, thereby defeating the constraining purpose of the legislature's adoption of formal rules in the first place. Thus, a judge like Keen, who himself believes in the subservience of judges to the legislature, would want to adopt a formal methodology to help ensure that subservience for himself, and even more so for his fellow judges.

The point here is not to evaluate the strength of an argument for formalism. An opponent of formalism could argue that its costs in terms of inflexibility are too high or that its claims of constraint are a façade because formal rules can be manipulated. Indeed, formalism is controversial, and we will return to its problems in due course. The point here is not to evaluate its propriety but merely to see that Keen's commitment to formalism is related to his commitment to a court's subservience to the legislature.

Keen's belief in the subservience of courts to legislatures is connected to an underlying political value: democracy. The connection here is quite obvious and straightforward: legislatures are organs of democratic expression. But jurisprudential positions can also be connected to underlying moral or political values in more complicated ways. For example, formal decision-making might further our ability to predict governmental action (because judges can consider only a limited number of facts) and thereby facilitate private decision-making through market transactions. This, in turn, reveals an implicit preference in the structure of legal reasoning to market transactions rather than to some other form of social organization. Some of the most insightful jurisprudential work uncovers heretofore unrecognized connections between the *structure* of legal reasoning and underlying political values. Much of the best work from the Critical Legal Studies movement, which we will discuss later, does this.[17] The point here is that different jurisprudential positions about institutions and methods invoke different underlying moral, political, and social values. Keen's jurisprudence reflects one such connection: a formal methodology that is driven by a commitment to the subservience of courts to legislatures that, in turn, is driven by a political commitment to democracy.

Keen's commitments to formality and to courts' subservience to legislatures are also connected to his insistence on a rigorous separation of law and morals. Moral values are the province of the legislature, not the courts. Moreover, courts should apply the law with reference only to facts triggered by the formal rule, not with reference to the myriad facts that might be relevant to a moral inquiry about right and wrong. Both of these commitments depend to some extent on a judge's ability to rigorously separate issues of law from issues of morals. A judge must be able to identify what law requires without reference to moral principles. Even if legal and moral norms overlap, the judge must be able to ascertain what the law requires without reference to moral norms.

Finally, all of this is connected to Keen's theory of interpretation. Although literalism—a theory that meaning can be gleaned from words alone—is, on the surface, different from formalism, the two concepts mutually reinforce each other. Formalism limits the judge's inquiry to facts designated by a (formal) rule. It must be possible to identify these facts without referring to the very considerations the formal rule was designed to prevent the judge from considering. Put another way, it must be possible for the judge to understand the *meaning* of the rule without referring to factors that the rule's formality was designed to opaquely screen from the judge's attention. Similarly, in order to maintain the separation of law and morals, it must be possible for a judge to ascertain what the law means without referring to moral concepts about what the law ought to mean. Literalism accomplishes both of these tasks.

Interpreting other sources of law, such as common law precedents, raises additional issues. An earlier court might state a "rule" that might be interpreted literally, just like a statute. But if the earlier court merely reached a result on given facts, literalism would not help. Some other method of interpretation would be necessary, and it would have to avoid referring to the judge's own sense of right and wrong.

A method of interpreting precedents akin to literalism is hard to imagine. It might entail applying a precedent only to identical facts, but the facts of a new case are always somewhat different. So what differences are relevant and thus can be used to distinguish the earlier case? There is no literal or mechanical way to know. Maybe Keen would insist on separating law and morals only when interpreting statutory law because that is necessary to be subservient to legislatures. We really do not know what Keen would say because he was not faced with a problem of common law interpretation. At the same time, he read *Valjean* broadly beyond its narrow facts, claiming that it undermined reliance on deterrence as the source of exceptions to the statute not only in cases of theft but also in cases of murder. But he "distinguished" the self-defense case by saying simply that the current case does not involve a claim of self-defense and that the issue there was whether the killing was "willful." All of this is not much to go on. The point is that, whatever method of interpretation Keen advocates for interpreting case law, it will affect and be affected by his other jurisprudential views about formalism, the institutional role of courts vis-à-vis other institutions, the source of law, and the relationship between law and morals.

HANDY IS AT THE opposite end of a spectrum from Keen. He is not as concerned as Keen is that courts should be absolutely subservient to legislatures. To be sure, he does not argue for the relationship to be the other way around, and he would not nominally refuse to follow the legislative command where it was clear and uncontroversial. But he sees courts and legislatures as being in the cooperative business of ensuring that legal disputes are resolved in accordance with public opinion and common sense. Like Keen, Handy invokes the will of the people, but the legislature is not the only body that can discover or express that will. Handy himself can ascertain the will of the people on a particular issue by referring to public opinion polls. At least compared to Keen, Handy sees the courts and the legislature as partners in structuring legal solutions to fit shared values. Courts and legislatures might be somewhat distinct. Legislatures announce broad, general norms, and courts apply those norms to concrete factual situations. But the methodology to resolve difficult problems is not all that distinct: reach a result that comports with shared public values.

Handy's methodology is nonformal. The legal "rule" contained in a statute does not operate as an opaque screen to prevent judges from consulting policies or facts. Indeed, few if any relevant facts are beyond the appropriate consideration of the judge. Even information obtained from Handy's relative is relevant, and the criteria for reaching an appropriate result are similar to those for the legislator. Legal rules are not formal constraints on a judge; they are "tools" and "instruments" through which the judge should craft a morally and politically correct result.

Even for Handy, however, judges might have some formal restraints. On some issues—such as the election of officials—courts should follow formal rules establishing the basic ground rules of government. And even on "substantive" issues, some "facts"—such as whether the explorers gave money to charity—might be out of bounds, even though they are not strictly irrelevant to how the explorers deserve to be treated. So even for Handy, law poses *some* formal constraints on judging. We need not turn him into a caricature. But if Handy is not quite the equivalent of a kaid dispensing purely individualized "justice" to a nomadic tribe, he approaches the nonformal end of the spectrum of what it means to think like a lawyer.

The source of law for Handy seems to be the popular will, ascertained directly, not necessarily through the legislature. Law is not merely what a specific authoritative body, the legislature, says it is; it is also informed by the public ethos. Too much should not be made of this point. We have to be careful here. We do not know what Handy's views are about how a sheriff or citizen should ascertain her legal obligations. Should that person, too, consult public opinion, or would a *court's* decision be determinative? When all is said and done, Handy may be a staunch formalist when it comes to other officials interpreting *his* decisions. But at least when a judge is "thinking like a lawyer," law has many sources, including common sense and public opinion.

Handy is also less insistent than Keen in rigorously separating law and morals. Legal rules are instruments for reaching "morally" correct results. Handy does not espouse a special or detailed moral theory, but he is quite willing to consult his own pragmatic views of right and wrong to help him ascertain what the law means. True, he does not merely consult his *own* views about morality; he consults social and public perceptions of right and wrong. But either way, he does not consider law and morals to be entirely distinct realms.

Finally, Handy has a theory of interpretation that differs dramatically from Keen's. Words do not have clear, fixed meanings that can be understood purely literally by a reader. Words are used to achieve certain ends. They are tools to construct meaning; they do not carry little packages of meaning independent of their context. Words and concepts do not have a reality of their own; they are tools to be used pragmatically. Most important, they are inherently imprecise and fuzzy. For example, what precisely does it mean to take another human life "willfully"? Judges interpreting these words do not merely find meaning passively; they infuse the words with meaning in specific contexts.

AS WITH KEEN'S VIEWS, Handy's views on each of these specific issues hang together to form a coherent, elegant unit. Because law should not be formal, there is no need to insulate judges from a wide-ranging array of facts to decide the case. Any relevant fact or policy is a permissible tool for the judge to use. As a consequence, there is no need to insist on a rigorous separation of law and morals. Since the nonformality of a judge's method does not prevent reference to moral values and policies, those moral values and policies can themselves be thought of as part of the "legal" material a judge can consult.

All of this is supported by an institutional view that courts are not entirely subservient to legislatures but instead are co-equal partners (or nearly so) engaged in a common task: furthering shared values. Legislatures are not the only governmental bodies that can ascertain and speak to a community's (moral) values. Legislatures need not "control" the facts and policies to which judges refer in reaching decisions. Judges can consult the same types of facts and values available to a legislature. These moral values are not inherently outside of the law.

Handy's views about institutional roles, law and morals, and formalism are related to his theory of interpretation. Because there is no need to insist that judges refrain from considering certain facts or policies when interpreting and applying law, Handy need not insist that judges ascertain meaning by looking at words alone. He can recognize, indeed relish, the inherent ambiguity of words and their inherent flexibility of meaning. Because he is not estopped from considering all facts and policies in ambiguous situations, he can use these facts and policies to fill the words with meaning by fitting them to the factual and moral details of the case. Words should be interpreted pragmatically and used as tools to bring about justice. Interpretation is an active, not passive, process that uses words to achieve worthwhile goals.

Finally, Handy's views on these issues may reflect underlying assumptions about society and commitments to certain substantive values, although he is not explicit about this. His methodology gives judges more flexibility to tailor results to individual needs. To the extent that it makes it more difficult for citizens to predict what judges will do, Handy favors individualized justice over order and predictability. This, in turn, implicates other social values. To the extent that private ordering through market transactions is fostered by stability and predictability, Handy is less committed to the market. True, this case does not involve a market transaction, so it would be possible for him to have a different methodology for interpreting contracts. But to the extent we can generalize from this one opinion, his method of interpretation seems to de-emphasize the social desirability of order, stability, and (probably) markets.

Thus, like Keen's jurisprudence, Handy has a way of thinking about various jurisprudential issues in a way that has a certain integrity. His views fit together in a stronger unit than any of the individual parts.

FOSTER HAS JURISPRUDENTIAL views that are between Keen's and Handy's. Courts and legislatures have different jobs, and in performing its job a court is subservient to a legislature. Legislatures define the goals and ends to be served by law, whereas courts implement law in individual cases by keeping faithful to those ends and goals. But unlike for Keen, for Foster this is not a mechanical task. Courts are required to be faithful to the intent, goals, and values of the legislature, not merely to its words. A court cannot substitute its view of society's goals for that of the legislature, but it can investigate thoughtfully those goals to see how they can be best pursued in individual cases. Thus, courts are servants of the legislature by considering the values, goals, and ends the legislature was trying to achieve. Unlike for Handy, courts cannot make their own independent choice of the goals, purposes, and ends. Thus, courts are not doing the same job as legislatures. But neither are they thoughtless ciphers. They evaluate social goals and purposes, just not from their own perspective. They identify the goals and purposes defined by the legislature.

Courts have a different role from legislatures in yet another respect. They decide cases only within their *jurisdiction,* that is, within their competence to decide. A case in the cave is beyond that jurisdiction. The cave here is just a metaphor. There may be *types* of cases beyond the substantive jurisdiction of courts such as cases involving political questions that are best left to the other branches of government or nonjusticiable issues that call only for advisory opinions. In these types there are no real cases or controversies for courts to decide. Or, as we will learn later, cases may be beyond the substantive jurisdiction of courts because they involve certain types of complex social problems courts are ill-equipped to resolve.

Foster's method is more formal than Handy's but less formal than Keen's. For Handy, the statute does not screen any facts or social policies from a judge's consideration, whereas for Foster the law does screen out some values and purposes, that is, values and purposes other than those of the legislature. It also screens out any facts that are not relevant to the *legislature's* purposes, values, and goals. But unlike Keen's methodology, Foster's does not screen out reference to *all* policies, goals, and values, as would the words of a rule. The judge can still consider the policies, goals, and values underlying the legislature's acts, and he can consider any facts that are relevant to those policies, goals, and values, even if the rule itself does not mention them expressly. Specifically, Foster refers to the goal of deterrence even though the statute does not expressly refer to it.

The source of law for Foster is mixed. The prong of his argument that says the explorers were in a "state of nature," not in "civil society," admitted to the possibility that law can exist without a governmental command. A law of nature, as posited by contractarian moral and political theory, could be used to evaluate the conduct of the explorers. Thus, Foster paid homage to a "natural law" tradition that sees nature, not governmental command, as a source of law. Foster did not take a strong natural law position, however, because he thought "positive" law supplanted natural law when it applied.

Even when applying "positive law" in the second prong of his argument, Foster views law as having different sources from Keen or Handy. The sources of law include the "command" (statute) of the legislature, but they also include the underlying purposes, goals, and ambitions of those commands as they affect our social structure. Thus, the "spirit" of the statute is a source of law as much as the words.

Foster's position on the relationship between law and morals is also between Handy's and Keen's. Law and morals are not identical for Foster. The legislature can promulgate immoral laws, and yet they remain valid laws. One suspects that Handy might never reach a result he thought was seriously immoral. Foster, by contrast, might. But Foster does not agree with Keen that law and morals can be kept entirely separate. To ascertain what law means, Foster must consult what law *ought* to mean—at least from the perspective of the authors' values, goals, and ambitions. Foster does not consult his own moral values or even the moral values expressed in public opinion. But he does consult the moral goals and values of the authors of the statute to determine how to apply it in individual circumstances. Since a judge must (or should) consult moral values to apply law, law and morals are inextricably intertwined. They cannot, as Keen believes, be kept rigorously separate.

Foster's theory of interpretation denies that words carry clear, fixed meanings that can be ascertained passively by referring to the words alone. A judge—or anyone interpreting a command—must look beyond the words alone to the context, including the speaker's purpose. This is not just a "jurisprudential" view for Foster. His example of the parent's commands to the maid reveals that this is a general theory of how we understand language.

Justice Foster's theory of interpretation is also different from Handy's. For Handy, words are malleable instruments that can be used as tools to reach desirable results. Of course, unlike Humpty Dumpty, it is unlikely that Handy thinks words can be made to mean anything we want.[18] But if words are not infinitely malleable, they are at least very malleable, and ambiguities should be resolved in light of the *reader's* values, goals, and vision. For Foster, words can be malleable and ambiguous, but their meaning is informed by the *author's* values, goals, and vision.

As with Keen and Handy, the various aspects of Foster's jurisprudence resonate. Law and morals cannot be kept entirely separate because interpretation requires the reader to consult the goals and values of the author. Likewise, law cannot be entirely formal, because it cannot be applied without interpreting it, and interpretation requires a judge to consult facts, values, and goals that are not expressly identified by the words of the statute.

SO WHERE DOES all of this leave us? We began with a simple question: Should the explorers' conviction be affirmed or reversed? This exemplifies the task facing law students or anyone who is trying to think like a lawyer: What is the "correct" solution to a particular legal problem? What does the "law" require? This task, in turn, leads to the type of disagreement that often animates law school classrooms but that often is not brought to the surface: What is the appropriate *method* for ascertaining the "correct" legal solution? What precisely does it mean to think like a lawyer? This is not the only source of disagreement. Students often disagree about other facts and values. But this is often the source of disagreement. So this is the first lesson of "The Case of the Speluncean Explorers": how easy it is for a legal dispute to turn into a jurisprudential dispute, that is, into a dispute about legal reasoning itself. How can we know the "correct" result unless we know the correct "method" of reaching that result?

Keen, Handy, and Foster each had different approaches to what legal reasoning is. They disagreed about where law comes from, about formality, about the relationship of law and morals, about the institutional roles of courts and legislatures, and about modes of interpretation. Moreover, their answers cohered into jurisprudential camps, with their positions on certain issues resonating with their positions on others. The individual questions they faced are the core questions of jurisprudence. The three sets of answers (or "jurisprudential camps") they articulated represent in very rough form three of the most influential schools of thought in American jurisprudence: Legal Formalism, Legal Realism, and the Legal Process School.

Thus far, we have merely scratched the surface about these individual issues and the sets of answers that form coherent jurisprudential schools of thought. We will be returning to each of them in due course. The point here is that these jurisprudential questions and these jurisprudential schools of thought need not be invented from the outside. They are confronted quite naturally from within the practice of law by thoughtful practitioners of legal reasoning. They are the natural questions that confront judges and lawyers who reflect on their business.

SO WE HAVE RAISED a lot of questions, but what are the answers? Keen, Handy, and Foster recognize that to decide a specific case they have to choose a methodology. Each chooses a methodology he thinks is "correct." But now we have simply pushed the problem back one step. What is the proper method? More important, how do we go about the task of answering *that* question? Is there something *inherent* in the concept of judging that supports one method over the others? Is there something *inherent* in the way we understand language that prefers one method of interpretation? Is there something *inherent* in the nature of law and morals that supports or undermines their separation? In other words, are there metaphysical concepts about the world that *reveal* answers to these questions?

Or do these methodological questions themselves present the justices with political and moral choices? And if they do, who should decide them? Should each judge make his or her own decision, or should the legislature, constitution, or earlier courts resolve these methodological issues? How should judges go about interpreting what their own methodological obligations are? Can we ever arrive at firm ground? Are there ever going to be (even in theory) firm answers to legal problems based on firm methodology? Or is the methodological dispute itself subject to so much uncertainty and choice that legal analysis is inherently performed on shifting sands? Whatever the answer is in theory, it is clearly true in practice that law teachers disagree about method. These shifting and unanalyzed sands help make learning to think like a lawyer so difficult.

LET US TURN TO TATTING. In some ways he is the most interesting justice. He sees the problem. He is supposed to decide the case not merely on his own discretion but according to law. He cannot do this until he ascertains how he should go about deciding what the law is. But when he listens to his colleagues, he cannot decide which of them is correct about the proper method. Where is he to turn? The "law" cannot remove the awesome responsibility of deciding the explorers' fates unless it dictates a result, and it cannot dictate a result unless it prescribes a method. But each of his fellow justices gives compelling critiques of the others. If the method cannot be ascertained, how can he legitimately act at all?

Tatting poses a fundamental question for legal reasoning. Can thinking like a lawyer be put on firm ground, and if so, what are the criteria? Are they moral, empirical, or metaphysical? More important, if it cannot, where do we go from here? Should judges stop judging? Should we dispense with discourse that *purports* to engage in "legal" reasoning and just admit we are making existential choices? Or should we merely choose "our" method, disagree where we have to, and jump in and play the game? Should loss of conviction at the most basic level lead to paralysis? In many ways—and not only in law—this is a central question for what has come to be called our postmodern, self-reflective era. Hamlet would feel right at home.

Most people who read "The Case of the Speluncean Explorers"—and herein lies much of Lon Fuller's genius—nod approvingly at some portions of each opinion. Each seems to strike something of a chord, even if we end up preferring one method over the others. Do we trust Handy in his freewheeling approach? Can we tolerate Keen's seeming inflexibility? Can Foster really ascertain a law's "purpose"? Yet if we cannot firmly decide what thinking like a lawyer means, law will be forever built on a shaky foundation. A certain task of jurisprudence is to determine whether law—and therefore legal reasoning and the very concept of the rule of law—can be put on firm ground. And if it cannot, can we learn to live with the uncertainty? We shall come back to these issues. But we have much ground to cover before getting there. For now, we should take Tatting's paralysis seriously: If we cannot decide how to decide, what business do we have deciding in the first place?

In "The Case of the Speluncean Explorers," we see the central issues of jurisprudence from inside legal practice. From the simple question of what result to reach, we quickly confront questions about what it means to think like a lawyer. And we see at least some plausible schools of thought about that question. Not surprisingly, we shall see that these three schools of thought have had a dramatic influence on what it means to think like a lawyer and, therefore, on legal education. We can now turn to these issues in more detail.

THREE

LAW'S CONTOURS

WE NEED TO IDENTIFY some of law's interesting contours and their effects on social organization. This is not an attempt to give a pervasive definition of law. We will ask whether that is possible in chapter 4. For now we want merely to get a handle on some of the structural features law has that affect how we think about it.

The first feature most people notice about law is that it is coercive. If you run a red light, you can be fined. If you murder someone, you can be imprisoned. You are required to pay your taxes. And so on. Law often coerces us to do things we would not otherwise be inclined to do. We will discover in chapter 4 that coercion may not be a *necessary* feature of law. Sometimes law gives us opportunities that we can take or leave at our option, such as the opportunity to make a will or form a partnership. One of law's salient features, then, is that it is often coercive. But whether it is always and necessarily coercive is a matter of controversy.

A second structural feature is that law is often formal in the sense we saw in chapter 2. It uses rules that depend on less than all of the circumstances that might affect our normative decisions.[1] A trivial but instructive example is a law that requires us to stop at a red light. It is motivated by a purpose of protecting our safety and the safety of other drivers. It facilitates traffic by allowing us to rely on other drivers' stopping. But when we apply it, we do not apply all of the factors that promote driver safety. We do not look to see if there is traffic coming in the other direction. We do not ask how important it is to get to our destination. Both of these would be relevant in balancing safety with convenience. The rule selects a small subset of those factors. Indeed, it identifies one fact and one fact alone. Is the light red? Once that formal rule has been established, it is opaque to the reasons that generated it.

Not all laws are this formal. We sometimes use nonformal legal standards, such as the standard in personal injury cases that requires an actor must use "reasonable" care. This standard is not *entirely* nonformal. It does not allow us to take into account the moral worthiness of the actor, but it does not screen out very much relevant information. And we saw in chapter 2 that a legal *method* might be more or less formal. Later we examine why we might want more or less formality in our legal system. The point here is that law *often* uses formal rules.

A third feature is authority. Law often asks individuals to defer to an authority other than themselves, usually by using formal and coercive rules. Deference is usually shown to a centralized authority, but it need not be. We might have a system that requires each person to defer to the judgment of the person on their left. But in actual practice, our legal system usually asks us to defer our individual judgments to those of a central authority such as a legislature or a court. So this feature might also be viewed as centrality.

Max Brod was a longtime friend and confidant of Franz Kafka. When Kafka died, Brod was in possession of many of his unpublished manuscripts. Kafka left him clear instructions to burn all of the manuscripts. Fortunately, Brod ignored the instructions and published the works anyway. The interesting issue is that Brod felt it was necessary to write a postscript to the publication explaining why he had ignored Kafka's wishes.[2] One set of reasons focused on Brod's belief that Kafka didn't really mean it. Other aspects of Kafka's behavior seemed inconsistent with a genuine desire to have his works burned. But another part of Brod's explanation was that it would be too detrimental to the literary world to defer to Kafka's wishes. This may be an odd example of authority and centrality. Brod ultimately did not defer to Kafka's wishes. But the salient point is that he felt obliged to write a postscript to explain that. His decision was the "exception to the normal rule" that expects us to defer to the author's wishes on certain issues. His postscript demonstrates just how powerful the idea is that often it is our duty to "obey" the decisions of others.

There are other features we *might* want to attribute to law. Shouldn't it be objective? And determinate? And neutral to disagreements about the good life? Maybe. But these are contentious features that law might or might not have. We will have to wait for later to determine whether law actually achieves these goals. But coerciveness, formality, and authority (centrality) are features law clearly has just as a descriptive matter. So they will have to do for now.

WHY SHOULD WE accept and follow law? Why would we ever give up our own decision-making capacity by deferring to a formal, central, coercive order? There are many benefits, but there are also many problems. Some of these attractive and unattractive aspects of law are practical and technical, but some of them are emotional and existential. Examining them not only provides insight into the role of law in our society but also helps provide insight into the emotional reaction law students have to learning how to think like lawyers.[3]

THE MOST PREDOMINANT and obvious benefit of deferring to a formal, central, coercive order is that it helps us predict what other people will do. This, in turn, helps us plan our affairs to pursue our goals. If the state will enforce contracts, we can rely on them to pursue our own commercial interests. If we know that the state will protect our property, we can rely on the fact that we will own it in the future and invest in it to promote productivity. As a mundane example, would we fill up the gas tank of our car if we could not rely on the fact that we will own it tomorrow? Or would we drive through an intersection on a green light if we could not count on the cross traffic stopping at the red light?

Formality is especially important for providing predictability. It is difficult to predict what other people will do under nonformal standards. If our neighbors are told to be reasonable with respect to our property, we can't be sure what they—or later a court—will think is reasonable. Maybe it was reasonable for my neighbor to borrow my car when I was not using it. Nor can we count on cross traffic stopping if the command to them was to watch out and proceed with caution. Formal rules like "ownership" of my property or like the cross traffic will stop at a red light are much easier to predict.

Ted Turner understood the value of formality. He had purchased MGM and with it a large library of old movies to show on his television station. He decided to colorize some old black-and-white movies so that they would be more attractive on television. This was controversial in the artistic and film community. So, naturally, Congress decided to hold hearings to decide whether it needed to take action.

Typically, each member of the committee hearing the matter made a lengthy opening statement. What are we to do with this complicated issue? On the one hand, we have the interests of people who want to watch color movies on television. On the other, we have the interests of film purists who want to protect the "integrity" of classic black-and-white movies. Alas, how are we to go about balancing these interests? And then the chair of the committee turned to Turner. Why should you be able to colorize these movies?

Turner could have answered with a complicated analysis of competing interests. How should we balance these interests, nonformally and all things considered? But he took a different tack. He simply answered: Because I wanted to, and they are mine.[4] The formal role of ownership is easy, predictable, and efficient. The nonformal approach of considering all of the advantages and disadvantages is not. By definition, formality reduces the amount of information we need to process in order to make a decision. This is precisely why it enhances predictability. This is not to say that we have to agree with Turner. It is merely to highlight the contrast between formality and nonformality.

Formality contributes to predictability, but so, too, does authority (or centrality) and coercion. Centrality ensures that there is one rule. If every individual made her own rule, we wouldn't know which one to apply. Moreover, coercion gives us more confidence that other individuals will follow the rules.

A second advantage of a centralized set of formal norms is that it makes life easier because it reduces the amount of information we need to make a decision. Which car should I drive to work? The one in my driveway or the one in my neighbor's driveway? Which car gets the best gas mileage? Which will be easiest to park? Which will be the most fun to drive or the least expensive to operate? I could think about these questions every morning, or I can simply follow the formal rule that I don't own any of the other cars. By reducing the amount of information needed to make a decision, formal rules are easier to apply.

Centralized formal rules also help us share responsibility for difficult decisions. When a student asks me to waive the requirement to write a final paper or take a final examination, I could provide a lengthy explanation about how writing the paper or taking the exam will make her better off in the long run. Or I can simply say that the university's rules don't give me the authority to do that. When Abraham was about to kill Isaac, he could tell himself that it was God who told him to do it. Of course, there is another side to this coin, as there is for all of these features. It may not always be desirable to evade responsibility by deferring to authority, but sometimes it at least seems convenient. We often defer to social or legal rules to claim that a certain decision is not our "job."

Deferring to centralized, formal, coercive rules can also help us avoid errors. At first blush this seems odd because formality limits our access to relevant information. This should sometimes create erroneous decisions. Indeed, it might. But there are also important ways in which it can help us avoid errors. Individual decision makers might have biases that they want to protect against. Individual jurors embedded in a lawsuit might be too close to the situation to properly evaluate hearsay evidence, a confession that did not comply with Miranda warnings, or oral testimony about a contract that should have been in writing. When Odysseus tied himself to the mast, he did not trust the decision he would make under the influence of the Sirens' song. So he tried (unsuccessfully as it turned out) to prevent himself from making an individualized decision. A self-imposed rule at the supermarket that forbids a shopper from buying anything not on his shopping list (under the influence of an inviting aroma) does the same thing.

Individual decision makers might also be inept. What do I know about the effect of certain chemicals on the water table? When I defer to centralized, formal, coercive rules promulgated by the Environmental Protection Agency (EPA), I am more likely to get the right answer because people at the EPA are technically more knowledgeable.

In addition to ineptness and bias, we might not trust the values of certain decision makers. We could let all individuals decide for themselves whether to use any given car on the street, but we might be afraid that some of those individuals are just selfish thieves. The more we don't trust certain decision makers, the more we might want to avoid erroneous decisions by constraining them with centralized, formal, coercive rules.

In these situations, formality and centrality work together. If we decide that we want a central decision maker with, for example, the expertise of the EPA, it would be difficult to have the EPA decide every case without issuing formal rules. Merely telling people to "protect" the environment would defeat the purpose. Having the EPA adjudicate every individual case would be overwhelming.

Centralized rulemaking might also simply be more efficient. A decision maker has to gather information. Sometimes this is easy, such as when I ask myself whether I am hungry enough to eat. At other times, however, the information I need to make a decision can be quite complex, such as whether it would be worthwhile to take a certain medication. It would be quite cumbersome for every individual to gather all of this information. It is far more efficient for a centralized body to gather the information—possibly by holding hearings or doing research—and then promulgate rules that transmit the results to individuals.

Sometimes we might want to invest authority in a centralized body because of our commitment to a political theory. Democracy, after all, is a political theory that says the majority—probably acting through a legislative body—has political legitimacy to make certain kinds of social decisions. Or we might believe in the divine right of kings.

Centralized, formal rules can facilitate productive activity by establishing roles and practices. The rules of baseball don't just regulate the behavior of the players; they determine the behavior that constitutes playing the game. Rules do not prevent people from playing baseball; they create the very practice that allows people to play baseball. A score of music imposes rules, but it also creates a pattern of conduct that enables people to produce music. Legal rules that enable the formation of corporations, that enable the use of wills and trusts, that create negotiable instruments, and that establish the practice of contracting all make practices that create new opportunities for individuals. And we have legal rules that establish roles individuals play within the legal system, such as judges, trustees, partners, and guardians. True, the legal rules that establish these roles constrain the behavior of individuals who occupy them, but rules also create the roles themselves. Without them an individual would not have the opportunity to occupy the role. These rules create opportunities.

Consider the famous prisoner's dilemma.[5] Two thieves are caught and interrogated in separate rooms. The police try to get them to turn on each other. If one turns and the other doesn't, then the one who turns will be rewarded with a light sentence; the other will receive a heavy sentence. If both turn on each other, each will receive a sentence that is heavier than if he alone had turned but lighter than if the other alone had turned. If neither turns, then the sentence will be lighter than if the other turned or if they had both turned but heavier than if he alone had turned. The prisoners know all this. Here is a sample two-by-two matrix that displays these possible outcomes.

The prisoner's dilemma

		Thief 2	
		Stays Silent	*Betrays Thief 1*
Thief 1	*Stays Silent*	3 years / 3 years	0 years / 10 years
	Betrays Thief 2	10 years / 0 years	5 years / 5 years

Now given that the two prisoners are isolated from each other and kept from communicating and that each prefers a lighter to a heavier sentence, it follows that the rational thing for each to do is to turn on the other. Turning on the other is the rational thing to do because each must figure out what to do on the basis of what he thinks the other will do. Will the other keep silent, or will he turn? In either case, the prisoner sees that he will get a lighter sentence if he turns on the other than if he keeps silent. As the outcomes in the matrix show, he will get a walk rather than three years in the one case and five years rather than ten in the other. The upshot is that if both prisoners do what is rational, they will be worse off than if they acted contrary to what is rational.

The situation would be different if the prisoners could communicate with each other. Then they could make a binding agreement to keep silent. Such an agreement would in effect establish a rule that each would follow knowing that the other was bound to follow it, too, if they were caught and their captors tried to play each one against the other. It would thus lead to a better outcome than if they were left to choose what to do in isolation from each other. This is exactly what many legal rules do. They allow individuals to adopt precommitment strategies that will work to their advantage.

Legal structures also create practices that allow individuals to live for purposes larger than themselves. As Aristotle famously said, humans are political animals. We thrive not merely as individuals but as participants in a larger community. Legal structures create ceremonies that foster community participation, such as a change in office for the president or an attorney's taking the oath of office. They also create social roles that help individuals express their worth, such as by being a teacher, or a social worker, or an entrepreneur. The rules that define these roles, and the practices to which the roles belong, are not always legal. But they often are. In any event, they represent a feature of centrality that structures the world we live in. We would be atomized individuals without these roles and the practices to which they belong.

Centrally created social structures also help influence the forces that form who we become as individuals. We might decide that we want to eat healthy food but realize that it will be difficult to do so in certain surroundings, such as a bakery. We might want to structure the world so we can avoid these influences. We might want to influence the types of educational experiences our children have so that they will become certain types of citizens. A purely laissez-faire approach to society won't achieve this. That was Rousseau's view in *Emile.*[6] Indeed, Vladimir Lenin had something like this in mind when he argued for a dictatorship of proletariat that would lead to a withering away of the state.[7] But there are also more benign forms of structuring the social milieu to reinforce certain types of desirable characteristics in individual citizens.

Formal concepts can be useful by more efficiently organizing our understanding of the world. In the wonderful article "Tû-tû,"[8] Alf Ross describes a primitive island on which people react to a variety of situations—such as stepping on holy ground—with the idea that a condition called a "tû-tû" has been created. Then, the creation of a tû-tû has a variety of consequences, such as a person being prohibited from entering the dining hall, from participating in collective discussion, and so on. Our reaction is that this is a pure fiction or even superstition. There is no such thing as a tû-tû. But then we realize that our legal system does this same thing with regularity. A whole variety of different circumstances lead to a conclusion that someone "owns" an object, and then a whole variety of consequences follow that conclusion. The concept of "ownership" is as much of an intellectual artifact as is that of a tû-tû. But it is a very useful one.

Suppose that ten sets of circumstances lead to a conclusion of ownership (or a tû-tû) and that ownership (or tû-tû) in turn leads to fifteen different consequences. Without the intermediate concept of ownership (or tû-tû) we would need to describe 150 different relationships. Inserting the concept of ownership (or tû-tû) reduces that number to twenty-five. That is a pretty useful concept. We use these concepts in ordinary language. Law often creates them as well—for example, ownership, fiduciary duty, negotiable instrument, and so on. Ultimately, this function of law might reduce itself to the earlier benefit of predictability. By reducing the number of relationships we have to remember, it helps make the world more predictable.

We have already discussed some of the benefits of predictability, but there is a special place in Western political thought where predictability is particularly important: our commitment to liberty. By giving predictable and clear lines that define our liberties, a central, formal, coercive order makes them more valuable. If I know with some precision the extent of my right of free speech, I can exercise it with more confidence.[9]

This survey is not comprehensive. The point here is that these *structural* aspects of our legal system—what I have called "authority" (or "centrality"), "formality," and "coercion"—themselves have desirable consequences. Most debates about our legal system focus on its content. Is our tax system too progressive or not progressive enough? Should our environmental laws be stronger, or are they inhibiting our economy? And so on. But first-year students learning how to think like lawyers are learning about a legal system that also has these important structural aspects, irrespective of its content. We will spend more time evaluating them. For now, we simply want to introduce them.

WE HAVE FOCUSED on supposedly positive aspects of the structure of legal reasoning. There are negative aspects as well.

Formal rules do not perfectly map the policies that generated them into results. We might call this a "mapping error." When a motorist confronts a red light but there is no traffic on the cross street, the policy of avoiding accidents is not implicated, but the rule still requires the motorist to stop. This is not an unrelated side effect. The same formality that produced the desirable consequence of predictability is what causes it to make a "mistake." Predictability may be worth the "wasted" time the motorist spends at the red light, but in this individual case the rule still made a mapping error. All formal rules are like this. The statute of frauds, which requires certain contracts to be in writing, makes them more reliable, but there will be cases in which oral testimony is extremely reliable. That would be a mapping error.

Formal rules also freeze us in the past. A rule may have made perfect sense when it was adopted, but values change. Our predictions about the future often turn out to be wrong. So when we later apply the rule it might be out of sync with a desirable result. We might call this a "freezing error."

Freezing errors and mapping errors play a large role in introducing students to legal reasoning in the first year of law school. A common early discussion takes a nineteenth-century case and tries to apply it to a twentieth- or twenty-first-century setting. Maybe the most famous is *MacPherson v. Buick Motor Company.*[10] Mr. MacPherson bought a Buick from the dealer. It had a bad wheel that the manufacturer should have detected. This caused an accident, and Mrs. MacPherson was injured.

An old nineteenth-century case, *Winterbottom v. Wright,*[11] held that a person who negligently repaired a stagecoach could be liable only to the stagecoach owner, not passengers or bystanders. The rationale was that the repair person and the passenger or bystander were not in "privity of contract." If that rule were applied in *MacPherson,* she would not be able to recover from the manufacturer. Mr. MacPherson had privity of contract with the dealer, but not with the manufacturer. Mrs. MacPherson did not have privity of contract with either one.

This is a classic freezing error. The rule in *Winterbottom* was adopted when most commerce was face-to-face. By the time of *MacPherson* in the early twentieth century, much more of it was done through complex systems of distribution. And, of course, it was common for family units to purchase goods for each other. In an opinion by Justice Benjamin Cardozo, the court effectively abandoned the privity rule in a famous opinion that became a hallmark of legal education. We will examine his reasoning in more detail in chapter 5. It implicitly highlights the freezing problem that the very structure of legal analysis gave rise to and a heroic judge who was willing to remedy it. Someone trying to make a better case for formal rules might have chosen a case where hopeless ambiguity created havoc. At Columbia Law School, a mid-twentieth century center for skepticism about legal rules, *MacPherson* was the case that served as the focal point of the school's introductory teaching materials.

Earlier we saw that potential bias or lack of technical expertise of individual actors might make us worry about errors they would make in decentralized individual decisions. Thus, we might want to have a decision made centrally by people who are insulated from those biases or are more capable. But biases and capabilities might work in reverse. Decision makers in central bureaucracies have biases of their own. They might value their own jobs or the budgets allocated to their agencies. They might have a particular political perspective not shared by people in the field or, as we might say today, beyond the Beltway. They might be ignorant of particular circumstances in individual cases. Just as an individual company might undervalue the effect its effluents have on the environment, bureaucrats at the EPA might undervalue the effect a regulation has on productivity. A challenge for any legal system is identifying the best decision maker in any given area. We might agree that an individual restaurant patron is in a better position to determine what she wants for dinner, but it doesn't follow that central planners such as those at the Federal Aviation Administration are not in a better position to develop rules for air traffic control. And there are a myriad of cases in between. The political debate about governmental regulation and individual market decisions is often just such a debate. Identifying the best decision maker pervades debates about legal doctrine.

The debate about the role of duty in tort law, for instance, is a debate about whether juries or judges should decide certain matters in a personal injury case. Juries have a certain set of biases, typically owing to their sympathy with the injured individual in the case they are deciding. Yet judges have their own set of biases, typically owing to their favoring the overall system of justice and its effect on the economy. So an important task of our tort rules is to decide which set of biases is more appropriate for a particular issue.

We saw earlier that intermediate concepts like tû-tû or ownership can simplify our thinking about a complex problem by reducing the number of relationships we have to keep in mind. But there is a double-edged sword here. Once we give a name to a concept, we have a tendency to reify the concept and treat it as a metaphysical entity. Instead of taking the concept as a merely useful medium of thought, we come to think of it as a "real" thing, the unchanging meaning of the word or words we use to express it. But if we take the word or words we use to express a concept to have an unchanging meaning, this can lead to the same kinds of freezing errors that we discussed earlier.

The coercive nature of law also has a negative side. It can directly frustrate liberty and autonomy. Moreover, it can turn law into a dangerous tool if legal authority is put in the wrong hands. We don't have to look very far in history to see that a coercive centralized legal system, in the hands of a tyrant, can lead to disastrous results. Furthermore, we can become habituated to tyranny, which formality can facilitate because it is opaque to any facts or values not identified by a rule. These include the very facts and values that are necessary for evaluating our legal system. Applying rules formally can lead to blind and habitual obedience.

We saw that formal authority lets us escape responsibility. To be sure, we probably would go crazy if we had to take responsibility for every action we did. Surely we have the right sometimes to say that a decision is not our job. But if we get too comfortable with that, we can become callous to the fact that ultimately we are responsible for our actions. Formality tends to camouflage that fact. As Jean-Paul Sartre reminds us, Abraham cannot escape responsibility for his willingness to kill Isaac by saying that God commanded him to do it. It was Abraham who made the ultimate decision to obey God.[12]

Formality can also be alienating. Formal rules that take into account only a small portion of the facts cause us to interact as less than complete human beings. A popular T-shirt on college campuses in the 1960s said "Do Not Fold, Spindle, or Mutilate." This was a reference to the computer cards that were used to sort students administratively. The point was that we were more than mere numbers. In some relationships, we especially feel that we should engage with the whole person. We should engage "heart-to-heart." It doesn't feel like a proper family relationship to say that we don't care about the entirety of the person we are related to. However useful a prenuptial agreement might be, it seems to be antithetical to the nature of the relationship into which the parties are about to enter. At the same time, we don't want all of our relationships to be heart-to-heart. It would be awkward if every time we went into a supermarket the cashier asked about our entire life story. Our reaction would most likely be that we just wanted to check out with the greatest efficiency. The point is that the formality can be alienating, and *sometimes* this seems inappropriate.

One of the great themes of Greek mythology is the distinction between Apollo and Dionysus.[13] Apollo is cerebral, controlling, rational, and individualistic. He is Oedipus, alone and through reason, solving the riddle of the Sphinx. He is the god of the plastic arts that shapes the world. Dionysus is drunken, irrational, emotional, and communal. Apollo is transcendent. He is apart from the world and the group. Dionysus is immanent. He is part of the world and the group. The Greeks understood both of these postures. Law, as it turns out, is more Apollonian, both for good and ill. This is one of the reasons there is so much at stake in learning to think like a lawyer. Law affects practical aspects like predictability and mapping errors, but it also touches on very deep-seated issues of how we relate to our communities and to the world. We shall return to this issue in a moment.

SO LAW'S VERY STRUCTURE, not just its content, has consequences for social interaction. Some are attractive; others are not. Where does that leave us? We might make an overall determination that, *on balance,* some form of a formal, central, coercive legal structure is desirable. But we need not come to an all-or-nothing conclusion. It might be that formality, or centrality, or coerciveness is desirable in some areas of our lives but not in others. In some areas, we might value predictability very highly, such as in areas of economic activity and investments in property. In others, however, predictability might not be as important, such as in adjudicating the consequences of an auto accident after the fact. Or maybe mapping errors may be extremely important in child custody cases but not so important for our traffic laws. The alienating aspects of formality might be perfectly acceptable in faceless market transactions but not in our family lives. So it is not surprising that we have an eclectic system where law is quite formal, central, and coercive in some areas but not in others.

Moreover, the content of individual laws can be more or less formal, central, or coercive. Negligence law, for example, asks what a reasonable person would have done under the circumstances. That is a very nonformal legal standard. We might have legal rules that do not have any enforcement mechanism, thereby making them more hortatory and less coercive. Or we might have a legal standard that delegates authority to individual juries, making the system less centralized than, say, an environmental standard under which the EPA makes a final decision.

As we saw in chapter 2, it is not just legal *standards* that might be more or less formal. Our *methodologies* for interpreting law might be more or less formal as well. Justice Keen was more formal than Justice Foster, who in turn was more formal than Justice Handy.

Moreover, the marginal advantages and disadvantages of features such as formality are likely not to be uniform. If we find ourselves in a situation of great uncertainty, adding a bit of formality and thereby predictability may have a very high marginal value. As the world becomes more predictable, however, adding even greater predictability will have less marginal value. Conversely, the alienating aspects of being judged by an impersonal formal system may be lower in a society where there is already a great deal of heart-to-heart contact. But if society is already very alienated, adding more formal and thereby alienating relationships may be marginally more detrimental.

If we put all these factors together, we are likely to see an eclectic system that uses the "optimal" amount of law that is appropriate for a particular area. This will vary depending how fast values and conditions are changing, how important predictability is, how disastrous mapping errors are, and how well other nonlegal institutions regulate our culture. Indeed, it would mean that we would have a system very much like the eclectic system we actually have.

These considerations might also apply to our judgments about the appropriate method for judges to use. Maybe we would want a more formal method during some eras or in some areas rather than in others. Maybe a nonformal method is more appropriate in areas where we cannot tolerate mapping errors—for example, in applications of the death penalty. Or we might want a more nonformal methodology during eras of rapid change to avoid freezing errors. We might want a more formal method in eras or areas where it is more important to have predictability. Resolving these issues is not amenable to an easy calculus. Indeed, we should keep an open mind as we proceed forward with our inquiry. The point here is just that we are beginning to see some of the structural features law has and the impact they have on how law works in our society.

THESE ISSUES ARE of broader interest than just to lawyers. They pervade our culture. Consider Herman Melville's treatment of them in *Billy Budd.* Billy is the "Angel of God." He was taken off a merchant ship and impressed into the Royal Navy. He goes cheerfully, and he is a favorite of his new captain, Captain Vere, and of the rest of the sailors. He doesn't think too much about life; he just takes it as it comes. He is assigned to the highest point on the ship as the foretopman. His nemesis, John Claggart, is the sergeant at arms, who lives and works in the bowels of the ship. Claggart is a schemer who thinks too much about life. He falsely accuses Billy by spreading rumors that he is involved in planning a mutiny. When Billy learns about this from Captain Vere and has a confrontation with Claggart, he freezes. He has a stuttering impediment, so he cannot speak out to defend himself. Almost involuntarily, he strikes out with his arm and kills Claggart. This is a clear violation of naval discipline, so Captain Vere declares: "Struck dead by the Angel of God, but the angel must hang."[14] Why would we ever hang the Angel of God?

The trial setting takes place in Captain Vere's stateroom. We look out of the portholes, as though we were in Captain Vere's head. Claggart's body is on one side, and Billy is held in an anteroom on the other. We imagine two parts of Captain Vere's psyche competing for his allegiance. Does he uphold the order of naval discipline, or does he defer to the angelic nature of Billy Budd? After all, Billy wasn't trying to kill Claggart, and Claggart himself had falsely accused Billy. It would be grossly unfair to apply the letter of the law to hang Billy, but the Royal Navy is at war and has had to quell two recent mutinies. It is a classic spot between a rock and a hard place.

Vere argues to the members of the court martial that their allegiance is not to their own sense of justice, but to the King. "But do these buttons that we wear attest that our duty is to Nature? No to the King. Though the Ocean, which is inviolate nature primeval, though this be the element where we move and have our being as sailors, yet as the King's officers lies our duty in a sphere correspondingly natural? So little is that true that, in receiving our commissions, we in the most important regards ceased to be natural free agents. . . . Our vowed responsibility is in this: That however pitilessly [the King's] law may operate in any instance, we nevertheless adhere to it and administer it."[15] Vere's language is more poetic than the language of centrality, formality, and freezing errors, but he refers to many of the same ideas. Vere's reference to the King's image on the officer's buttons is just an argument for central authority. Vere's appeal to law rather than justice is an appeal to formality and to the separation of law and morals.

As it turns out, Melville was interested in how legal structures operate. His father-in-law, Lemuel Shaw, was an extremely prominent judge in Massachusetts in the early and middle part of the nineteenth century.[16] He was instrumental in bringing legal principles in line with the needs of a burgeoning proto-industrial economy, and he used flexible, policy-oriented reasoning to accomplish those ends. He decided a fugitive slave case where, much to his consternation, he was forced to send an escaped slave back to his owners.[17] Reportedly, Melville and Shaw discussed questions of this sort after dinner.[18] They are a central theme in Billy Budd. They resonate with lawyers and nonlawyers alike.

Billy Budd puts in stark relief some of the issues we have discussed. Where do we need order, discipline, and predictability more than on board a naval ship during time of war, especially when there have been recent mutinies? But hanging the Angel of God is a grotesque mapping error. We all know that the handsome sailor did not pose any real threat of mutiny.

Billy Budd goes beyond these pragmatic considerations. It puts in stark relief the more essential aspects of imposing a formal, coercive, central legal order on social life. Who is Billy? He is the foretopman at the highest point of the ship. His opposite is Claggart, the sergeant at arms, who works in the bowels of the ship. Billy lives his life without analyzing it. He is simple. He hides nothing. He has the happiness of a child. He is neither conceptual nor cunning. He has no guile. He represents immanence by being part of the world in an unreflective way. Claggart, by contrast, is planning and calculating. He hides his past. He has guile and is manipulative. He is apart from the world and is alienated. He is transcendent. With some irony, Billy is Dionysian immanence. Claggart is Apollonian transcendence. There is irony because Billy literally transcends the ship as foretopman, whereas Claggart is immanently within the ship as sergeant at arms.

Part of the brilliance of the Greek drama is that it recognizes the importance of both Apollonian and Dionysian aspects of the human psyche.[19] Only by balancing them can we live a healthy life. Captain Vere thinks he has to choose. His inability to reconcile this conflict haunts him until his death. His dying words are about the handsome sailor.[20]

THIS TENSION IS RAMPANT in Western literature and philosophy. Friedrich Nietzsche raises it in the *Birth of Tragedy from the Spirit of Music.*[21] We see it in the tension between classicism and romanticism, where classicism embodies form, order, and reason, and romanticism emphasizes substance, energy, freedom, and emotion. We see it in William Blake's juxtaposition of the Tyger and the Lamb.[22] We see it in James Fenimore Cooper's *Leatherstocking Tales,* where the Judge and Natty Bumppo complement each other.[23] With our cities filled with concrete, it is easy for us to valorize unspoiled nature.

But in the wilderness of upstate New York, the Judge could valorize carving a bit of order out of the wilderness. We see it in a film like *Dirty Harry,* where the protagonist must fight bureaucratic rules to achieve justice.[24]

Apocalypse Now[25]—and of course Conrad's *Heart of Darkness*[26]—is a brilliant exploitation of this tension. At the outset, we encounter stuffy and even prissy officers having tea in the middle of the war. They seem highly artificial and stylized. We don't much like them. As we proceed up the river in pursuit of Kurtz, we move from this stylized and artificial culture into nature. We take a journey from classicism into romanticism. At first it seems welcome, as when we encounter Robert Duvall's character surfing just before a helicopter attack and then playing Wagner from the helicopters as the attack proceeds. But as we get farther and farther up the river, and farther and farther from civilization, all of this becomes less attractive. Kurtz has abandoned any semblance of civilized order. It is instructive that we see Fraser's *The Golden Bough* on Kurtz's side table.[27] At this point the prissy and artificial culture of afternoon tea seems a lot more attractive.

In *1984* we are oppressed by the collective.[28] But when we encounter Dr. Zhivago hiking through the snow-swept Russian steppes, individualism seems lonely.[29] In *War and Peace,* Bezukhov thinks he can find the meaning of life through intellectual inquiry, taking up one intellectual "ism" after another, but when he is captured in the field by Napoleon's army, he learns from a peasant that the meaning of life is found in the day-to-day living of it.[30]

In Albert Camus's *The Artist,* the protagonist spends weeks trying to perfect one painting.[31] When he dies, his friends rush to see what he had accomplished. They are disappointed, because he seems to have painted a single word, but they can't make it out to be either "solitaire" or "solidaire." Aha! Adam and Eve before The Fall are one with nature and with God. But after they gain knowledge by eating the apple, they think too much about the world and become separated from God. They become thinking, rational, and self-conscious beings.

We have a promise of reconciliation only through a Messiah (or Christ). In Middle Eastern mythology, Gilgamesh has to choose between the pearl of wisdom and humanity.[32] (He chooses humanity.)

In Walker Percy's *The Moviegoer*, the protagonist thinks too much about life.[33] At one point he is on a train. He has many worries, including whether he should be running off with his cousin. He is constantly engaged in an internal conversation, mulling over all his problems. He notices that other people on the train are laughing, chatting, and just enjoying the moment. Why can't he do that? His overthinking the world alienates him from it. So he asks: Do I know something they don't know, or vice versa?[34] Claggart might ask the same question. It would have never dawned on Billy.

The theme of this tension is pervasive in our culture. It is a tension between two postures for relating to the world and to each other. We can be roughly Apollonian, or we can be roughly Dionysian. We can be Billy or Claggart. Legal reasoning asks us to take one side of this dichotomy. It is not surprising then, that it raises high stakes.

So law presents us with pragmatic choices between features like predictability and mapping errors. But it also presents us with fundamentally different postures toward life. So when a first-year law student is confronted with a hypothetical, there is a lot at stake, more at stake than appears on the surface. When asked whether a contract with seemingly unfair terms should be enforced against an impoverished widow, a student is being asked to take a particular posture toward life. Should the Angel of God be hanged? It is not surprising that this is an uncomfortable task. Not only is the material hard; it is psychologically disturbing in just the same way that Greek tragedy is psychologically disturbing. Sophisticated lawyers and law professors may take all of this in stride, but for many first-year law students, it can be new territory.

An Athenian watching a tragedy by Sophocles was torn between admiring an individual, self-reliant hero like Oedipus and the communal, traditional chorus.[35] It was designed to be a cathartic experience. A first-year student who faces a choice between the order of law and the empathy of individual justice faces a similar dilemma. If this has been a cathartic experience in Western literature from Greek tragedy until now, is it surprising to find that first-year students struggle with it?

How many contracts teachers look out at their class and see the audience of Oedipus?

FOUR

LAW AND MORALS: POSITIVISM AND NATURAL LAW

JUSTICES KEEN, HANDY, AND FOSTER disagreed about what law "is." What is its source? Is it something we "find" in nature, or is it purely a human artifact? How can we define what it is? Can we define it without reference to its moral content, that is, whether it is "good"? More generally, what is the relationship between "law" and "morals"? Are they synonymous? Are they entirely separate normative systems? Or is their relationship more complex?

Keen thought that law is entirely a human artifact. It is what an official governmental body says it is. Keen would undoubtedly recognize human sources of law other than the legislature, such as earlier court opinions or executive branch regulations. But in all cases, law is entirely a creature of official governmental edicts. It is a human creation. It is not something that we discover in nature (except, of course, that humans themselves are part of nature).

For Keen, law is entirely separate from morals. This affected his method of ascertaining the meaning of law: judges should look only to the pronouncements of governmental bodies. They should not look to their own or to society's independent moral values. If Newgarth's statutes mandated immoral results, the legislature should change the statute, not the court. What the statute says and what it ought to say are entirely separate questions. To ensure that judges adhere to this separation, they should not look to material beyond the words the legislature used to express itself. Looking to "public opinion" (as did Handy) or to a vague legislative "purpose" (as did Foster) wandered into the realm of "morals," not law. So the question of what law *is* and how judges should *act* are intertwined.

For Handy, there is no boundary separating law from morals. The words of the statute are "tools" to get to the "proper" result as defined by the public's view (and presumably by Handy's own view) of a proper result. Morals are a source of law, as is any other area of normative thought that bears on deciding how best to resolve the dispute in the case. When Handy consults public opinion or any other normative source to guide him in getting to a "correct" result, he is not stepping outside of the law; he is merely drawing on one of the indefinitely many ingredients that can go into determining what the law is. As with Keen, Handy's views about what law is and about legal method are intertwined.

Foster's views about the source of law and the relationship between law and morals are more complex. In part of his opinion, he claims that the "human" law of Newgarth is inapplicable in the cave, so the parties have returned to a "state of nature." There is a source of "natural law" that is independent of human edicts. But this law is supplanted by human law when the state of nature is replaced by civil society. We will return to these issues later.

For our current purposes, Foster's second prong is more interesting. Even under Newgarth's murder statute, the spelunkers' cannibalism is not murder because it does not implicate the purpose of the statute: deterrence. Foster does not think law is identical with morals. He does not think that what law *is* is identical to what law *ought* to be. The legislature can depart from what Foster thinks is just, and Foster will still enforce it. But neither are the law and morals entirely separate. In interpreting what the legislature meant, Foster needs to consult more than just the legislature's words. He needs to consult the legislature's moral purposes and goals.

To ascertain what law is, a judge has to evaluate what the *legislature* (not what the judge or God) thinks the law ought to do. "Is" and "ought," and "fact" and "value," are not entirely distinct. By consulting our legal system's goals and purposes, a judge is consulting "law" because those goals and purposes are part of law. Or maybe it is the other way around: because a judge must consult those goals and purposes to ascertain what the law is, these (moral) goals and purposes must be part of law. So for Foster, legal method and what law is are intertwined.

THESE THREE POSITIONS about the source of law and the relationship between law and morals roughly define three historical schools of thought. Keen's position is called "positivism": law is a purely human (governmental) artifact and is entirely separate from morals.[1] As a philosophical position, it is aligned to methodologies in other disciplines that call for careful analysis of surface behavior without "inventing" unseen, mysterious forces beneath the surface. Behaviorism in psychology is an example.[2]

Handy's position is called "pragmatism": law is an instrument of government to be used to promote the good of the community. It is neither closed off to morals nor limited in its reach by morals. Pragmatism is oriented toward achieving results that serve the interests of the community. To achieve such results necessitates attending to public opinion in determining what the law is in a given case, for no result the community would reject would serve its interests. The preferences of the people governed by law are, therefore, something a pragmatist judge heeds in determining the law. Pragmatism, as a philosophical position, is thus akin to utilitarianism, which determines the right action or policy by consulting the preferences of all those whose interests will be affected.[3]

Foster's position is a version of "natural law." Law is "out there" in the natural world even without governmental edicts. That is, law exists in nature itself, without any action by humans. It might have been imprinted on nature by God. Something like this is Foster's view in the first prong of his argument, where he speaks of law in the state of nature. A judge could ascertain this "law" and apply it without reference to legislative acts. Or, maybe, legislative acts contrary to the law of nature are not law at all. This theory has the burden of describing how a judge can ascertain the content of this natural law. Usually this is by exercising reason,[4] but it could be through revelation.[5]

Foster presents what might be called a "neo-natural" law position in the second prong of his argument. Law does not exist in nature itself or even in society absent governmental edicts, but neither is it entirely separate from having moral purposes. This is because a judge must refer to the legislature's (moral) purposes in order to ascertain the law the legislature intended when the words of the statute it enacted are ambiguous.

QUESTIONS ABOUT THE relationship between law and morals are addressed by philosophers more than by today's lawyers. True, judges and lawyers have to determine what they are supposed to refer to when they apply law, but this is usually implicit. Today's law students do not seem to worry much about it. If you ask them what law is, they will usually say something like, "The stuff we learn in law school." This is much like Justice Potter Stewart's view about hard-core pornography: he might not be able to define it, but he can recognize it when he sees it.[6] By and large, today's law students are positivists. They are quick to criticize law from an (external) moral perspective, but they don't claim it is not law.

Philosophers, however, often want a rigorous definition of law. Is it an autonomous discipline, or is it a subset of morals, politics, or economics? In any event, the debate between positivism and natural law has been a central question of legal philosophy for centuries.[7] We can now turn to it in more detail.

THERE ARE TWO BASIC strands of the natural law tradition. The first is that moral values are themselves embedded in nature, usually by God.[8] At first blush, this is a claim about ethics, not about our legal system. According to this theory, morality is discovered in nature, usually through the faculty of natural reason[9] (or maybe through revelation); it is not invented by humans. The second strand, which is a matter of jurisprudence or legal theory, is that the laws of our legal system are identical to those natural law moral principles.[10] Put another way, a human attempt to make law that is contrary to morals is not law at all.

These two strands of the natural law tradition—the ethics version and the jurisprudential version—usually go together, but they need not. A person might believe that ethics are found in nature—even created by God—but that human law is altogether separate. Or, to the contrary, a person might believe that ethics are entirely a human or cultural creation but that what we call "law" is entirely coincidental with those cultural ethical norms. It is the jurisprudential version of natural law—that "law" and "morals" (wherever morals come from) coincide—that interests us.

We need not survey all of the specific versions of various natural law theories other than to note some of the main proponents throughout history: Cicero[11] and the Stoics,[12] Hooker,[13] Grotius,[14] Pufendorf,[15] Locke,[16] and especially Aquinas[17] and Blackstone.[18]

AN INTERESTING FEATURE of the jurisprudential version of natural law is that it is both conservative and revolutionary. If something really is "law", then it is automatically moral, so there is no moral room to critique it. If it is not moral, however, it is not law at all, and there is no "legal" obligation to obey it.

In American legal history, the most influential proponent of natural law influence was probably William Blackstone, who published his *Commentaries* in England in 1765. (Coke's *Institutes,* published in England in 1628–1644, were also still very influential.) For Blackstone, a law that contradicted natural ethics was no law at all. We see a strand of this in the Declaration of Independence, with its "unalienable" rights,[19] that is, natural rights that cannot be alienated (given up) in civil society no matter what civil law tries to do. We still see echoes of this tradition as recently as Dr. Martin Luther King Jr.'s "Letter from Birmingham Jail."[20] He argues that there are two kinds of laws: there are just laws and unjust laws, and unjust laws are no law at all.

Even in Blackstone, however, we see aspects of positivism. It seems obvious in a modern society that some laws, like the tax rate or other technical regulatory laws, are not instinctively embedded in the universe or even in our cultural ethics. For Blackstone, the natural law has lacuna where human positive law can fill in details[21]. Surely Dr. King believed that too. And it would be hard to find a law teacher or student today who thinks the tax code is not "law" simply because they think it sets the wrong tax rate. Like Blackstone, we live in at least a partially positivistic age.

POSITIVISM, TOO, HAS ancient origins. It is chiefly associated with the Sophists. Plato, in Book 1 of *The Republic,* had the Sophist Thrasymachus put forward and defend the proposition that justice was what benefits the powerful.[22] This proposition and its corollary that laws were no more than conventions were among the Sophists' signature doctrines. But our interest is in the modern tradition of positivism. It begins with Jeremy Bentham's *A Fragment on Government* in the eighteenth century.[23] Bentham, in this work, attacked the natural law framework of Blackstone's exposition. His chief target was the idea of a social contract as the foundation of government, which Blackstone, following John Locke, based on natural law and natural rights. In Locke's version of the idea, some natural rights persist into civil society.[24] They are not alienated in the social contract. Thus we get Thomas Jefferson's "unalienable" rights in the Declaration of Independence.[25]

Bentham thought the idea of a social contract was a useless fiction. Government, he held, takes root when the members of a society come to have a habit of obedience to the will of a single individual or an assembly of individuals. Law, he maintained, is the expression of this individual's or assembly's will. Therefore, all law in the society is positive law. No law originates independently of the will of the individual or assembly whom the members of the society habitually obey, and the will of this individual or assembly need not reflect or be guided by moral principles.

Locke's version of the social contract theory was not the only version. Before Locke, Thomas Hobbes had based his political theory on a social contract in which humans (hypothetically, not historically) exchanged the freedom and natural rights they possessed in the "state of nature" for the security of civil society.[26] In chapter 7, we will return to other versions of social contract theory, such as Rousseau's, Kant's, and Rawls's. They will be important in their own right when we examine whether our legal system is morally legitimate or whether citizens have a moral obligation to obey the law. For our current purposes, however, the point is that, for Bentham, civil society and its laws are not founded on a contract that humans make by exchanging natural rights that existed in a state of nature. Bentham was a staunch positivist.

But now we have a new issue: How can we recognize or define what constitutes "positive law" in civil society? Would any norm count? Grammar? Manners? The rules of baseball? Can we define or recognize positive law without referring to moral principles, which would defeat the point of separating law and morals? The natural law tradition had its own issues. If the law of nature is the same everywhere, how can we account for the variety of laws in different jurisdictions? How can we access the natural law? And so on. But in the modern era, detailed questions about positivism have dominated the debate.

Bentham addressed this problem by saying that law is an expression, through the use of signs, of the will of the sovereign.[27] Put more succinctly, laws are the commands of the sovereign. This has a ring of plausibility. A legislature (sovereign) prohibits murder (a command). But issues arise about who counts as the "sovereign" and what counts as a "command." Bentham defined a sovereign as "any person or assemblage of persons to whose will a whole political community are [disposed] to pay obedience." [28] This makes a sovereign a political superior. This is problematic. Is an American state not a "sovereign," or is its legislature's enactments not "law," merely because it is not clearly a "political superior" to the federal government? States are superior on some issues but inferior on others. So, there is still work to be done.

The important point about Bentham's approach is not whether it is satisfactory (it seems clearly to fall short), but that it starts a tradition of trying to define law in purely non-moral terms. At least defining law as a "command" of a "sovereign" does not ask whether the content of the edict is good or bad.

JOHN AUSTIN, WHO was Bentham's disciple, wrote *The Province of Jurisprudence Determined*[29] in 1832. It, too, presents an attack on Blackstone and his idea of natural law. Its main goal is to carve out legal theory as something separate and distinct from ethics.

For Austin, law is a command from a political superior to a political inferior.[30] This is similar to Bentham. At the same time, Austin's account of these concepts was more accessible and differed in detail. It became the definitive statement. A "command" is "the expression or intimation of a wish" that carries a threat of a negative sanction if the wish is not complied with.[31] A speed limit of 70 miles per hour fits this definition. The legislature in enacting the law expresses its wish that drivers not drive at speeds exceeding 70 miles per hour and threatens to impose a negative sanction on those who do not comply. But what about patent law, or property transfers, or wills? They enable us to do things. There are no negative sanctions if we do not avail ourselves of them. Austin seems to have criminal law in mind, or maybe tort law. There are attempts to fit areas like patent law into this definition: you lose the benefits of a patent if you do not comply with the rules. But nothing requires you to get a patent. Still, even if Austin's definition falls short, it does capture an important feature of law we have seen before: law is often, if not always, coercive.

The second issue for Austin is who counts as a "sovereign." What about a gunman? Or today we might ask, Nazi Germany? Surely certain entities do not count, but Austin can't identify them by asking if they are "legitimate." That looks like a moral standard, which would defeat the very purpose of separating law from morals. So the answer for Austin is factual: a sovereign is habitually obeyed by the bulk of the population in a geographic area but does not habitually obey others.[32] That is not a moral definition. It might include the law of Nazi Germany; it would exclude a football coach. A football coach habitually obeys others. A church (in modern times) is not habitually obeyed in a geographic area, and it habitually obeys the state. (Maybe the medieval Catholic Church did promulgate law under Austin's definition.) But what about state and federal governments? They "obey" each other, depending on the issue. Or separation of powers? The legislature "obeys" the courts on constitutional matters, but the courts obey the legislature on the tax rate.

But even with these problems, Austin advances the ball. He identifies nonmoral attributes that law often possesses, and he continues the effort of trying to define "law" without reference to "morals."

OLIVER WENDELL HOLMES was not primarily a legal philosopher, but he announced a pithy and influential description of positivism. To understand our *legal* obligations, we should ask what a bad man would ask.[33] What obligation does a party to a contract have? We might say she made a promise, so she has an obligation to fulfill it. For Holmes, that would be moralistic. The "bad man" would see two options: he could fulfill the contract and avoid paying damages, or he could breach the contract, the promise, and pay damages. So he has a "legal" obligation to fulfill the contract *or* pay damages. The law is indifferent. Neither choice has a privileged position. To say that there is a legal obligation to fulfill a contract is moralistic.

Holmes does not improve on Bentham's or Austin's definition of law, but his "bad man" metaphor helps in clarifying what it means to purge moral concepts from our understanding of what law is.

OUR PENULTIMATE POSITIVIST is Hans Kelsen, who wrote *Pure Theory of Law* (a theory uncontaminated with moral concepts) in 1934.[34] Kelsen defined law as a norm in a system of norms that uses coercion to secure compliance. He held that the meaning of a norm is expressed in a statement about what ought to be done. "Slower traffic ought to keep to the right" expresses a norm. Why isn't "ought" a moral concept, which would give up the ghost? Kelsen avoids that trap by saying the norm "ought" to be obeyed not morally but because it is a *valid* norm in a *valid system* of (legal) norms.[35] A particular law ought to be obeyed because a higher legal norm validates it, the higher norm is in turn validated by an even higher legal norm, and so on. A law against murder is a norm passed by the legislature. A higher norm (say, Article I of the Constitution) says norms passed by Congress are valid. Ultimately, there is a basic norm, what Kelsen calls the "Grundnorm,"[36] that validates the entire system. In the United States, this would be something like an allegiance to the Constitution and the system of federalism it establishes. The Grundnorm is posited as a logically necessary basis for the system. It is never "justified" or derived. The test of a particular law's validity is *within* the legal system the Grundnorm generates.

A resulting legal system might be static (like the Ten Commandments) or dynamic (like "obey the King"). The American legal system is dynamic, with a complicated Grundnorm of constitutional allegiance. Kelsen then adds an empirical constraint: for a legal system to exist, it must be "by and large" effective.[37] This is added so a totally fictional system will not count. It is similar to Bentham's and Austin's requirement of a political superior—someone or some assembly of people who the whole community is disposed to obey or who the bulk of the population habitually obeys.[38] [39]

Kelsen's approach has an advantage over Austin's. A federal court does not fit Austin's definition of being habitually obeyed but not of habitually obeying others. Federal courts sometimes are obeyed by state courts, but on other issues they must themselves obey state courts. Sometimes a legislature obeys a court, but on other issues a court obeys a legislature. Kelsen's definition avoids this problem. The holdings of a federal court are valid norms in a valid system of norms because their force is defined by a valid system of norms underwritten by a complex Grundnorm of American constitutionalism. Similarly, the laws of wills and of contracts, which do not fit well into Bentham's or Austin's theory of "commands," are valid norms in a valid system of norms.

Kelsen's theory seems to be incomplete because to get it going we have to *presuppose* the Grundnorm. Why do that? Why not derive it? One answer is that we presuppose axioms in geometry without deriving them, and doing so yields a robust system of theorems. Moreover, Kelsen probably captures the intuition of most lawyers and law students. When asked why the rule against murder is a "law," they likely will say because the legislature said so. And why can the legislature say that? Because the constitution says so. And why is that? Well, that is just the way things are. You are asking too many questions. In fact, we do seem to "presuppose" the validity of our legal system and then identify as law those norms that it produces.

OUR FINAL POSITIVIST is H. L. A. Hart, who wrote *The Concept of Law* in 1961,[40] following his delivery of Harvard's Holmes Lecture, "The Separation of Law and Morals," in 1958, which was published that year in the *Harvard Law Review*.[41] Lon Fuller published a spirited reply in the same issue.[42] We will turn to Fuller's reply in due course. Hart follows Austin and Kelsen but tries to improve on their weaknesses.

Hart objects to Austin's reliance on "commands" (expressions of a wish backed by sanctions), because it doesn't capture laws like the First Amendment, or laws creating offices, or laws enabling transactions like contracts and wills.[43] He also objects, as did Kelsen, to Austin's formulation of a "sovereign" who is habitually obeyed but does not habitually obey others.[44] Even the King in England was "bound" by the Magna Carta, not to mention that the American Congress sometimes obeys the courts or the Constitution. And he is unsatisfied with Kelsen's merely positing the Grundnorm.[45]

So Hart says law is the "union of primary and secondary rules"[46] that the membership of a political society generally, and for the most part, follows. Primary rules govern people's behavior, such as the law of negligence or the tax code. Secondary rules tell us how the primary rules come about. Common law courts promulgate the rules of negligence, and the legislature sets the tax rate. Higher secondary rules tell us how lower secondary rules come about, such as when Congress delegates authority to the Internal Revenue Service and the Constitution empowers Congress to make laws. So far, this is a lot like Kelsen. And we still need an ultimate rule to get the whole process going.

For Kelsen that was the Grundnorm, whose validity was logically presupposed. For Hart, it is the "Rule of Recognition."[47] In the United States, the Rule of Recognition is something like a complex commitment to our constitutional structure. But whereas Kelsen's Grundnorm exists as a sine qua non, Hart's Rule of Recognition exists as a matter of *fact*.[48] A sociologist or anthropologist can look at how a culture actually behaves and identify its Rule of Recognition, just as a biologist can look at the behavior of bees and conclude that they "obey" the queen.

For Hart, we can identify law (and therefore the realm of legal study) as a factual phenomenon in the social world without referring to morals. This allows us to separate law from morals as a subject of study. It delineates the source of law for judges and other officials interpreting it. It sharply distinguishes an individual's moral duties from their legal duties. Responding to an objection to positivism that its conception of law as separate from morals leads people, especially judges, to accept evil laws and lose sight of the moral duties with which they conflict, Hart claims that a clear separation of law and morals actually focuses individuals (and judges) on the point that they may have moral obligations that are different from their legal obligations.[49] The mere fact that something is "legal" does not make it "moral."

As we shall see, there are problems with Hart's formulation, but it does reflect a certain amount of common sense. Most people today think a law might be morally bad, but it is still a law. Law students enter law school thinking something along the lines of "law is what the legislature says it is." Indeed, they often have trouble thinking that a reckless driver violated the "law" if there is no legislation. Their confusion is that they have too simple a Rule of Recognition. Then they internalize the idea of common law, so law can also be what courts say it is. Later they will see agency rules, conflicts involving federalism, and so on. They are just learning that Hart's Rule of Recognition is complex. But they are basically positivists. They think law is what some complex system of legal institutions says it is.

But many law students also express the same complaint as the objector to whom Hart replied.[50] Separating law and morals makes us insensitive to how the cases "ought" to come out, that is, insensitive to a more robust sense of social justice. Like the Sophists, lawyers as positivists are skilled at arguing to win, but they should also be attending to the moral high ground. This was Socrates's complaint. Hart would counter that lawyers should be interested in justice, but they should not be confused that law and justice are the same thing.

We will return to this point later. It is worth noting here that this is a psychological point, not an analytical one. Which approach will put individuals in the right frame of mind to be sensitive to justice in the world? It would be interesting to do psychology experiments to find out. Hart's claim is just that it might be (indeed, he thinks it is) an empirical fact that a rigorous separation of law from morals focuses our attention on our independent moral obligations. It does not suppress them. But the point here is not to resolve these particular psychological points.

It is noteworthy that students who do not want to exclude moral inequity from legal analysis do not retreat to a strong natural law theory by claiming that a bad statute is not law. They do not return to Blackstone. They may claim that law school *pedagogy* should focus more on social justice, but they do not attack the analytical separation of law and morals. Indeed, their complaint that American law is contrary to social justice presupposes this very separation.

AFTER WORLD WAR II, a new "neo-natural" law theory emerged, mainly from Lon Fuller and Henry M. Hart at Harvard. Fuller was concerned that positivism facilitated judges in Nazi Germany to enforce horrendous laws.[51] Had they considered the grotesquely brutal ends that those laws advanced, they might have had second thoughts. Positivism functioned like moral blinders. H. L. A. Hart, as we saw, disputed this. But no doubt, the behavior of positivist German judges during the Nazi era was an embarrassment to positivism, and this was one of the reasons Fuller thought law and morals *shouldn't* be separated even if they could be. And he thought that we can't fully separate them even if we wanted to.

Fuller makes his arguments in *The Morality of Law,* first published in 1964,[52] and in his reply to Hart's Holmes Lecture in the *Harvard Law Review.*[53] First, law by its very nature has an "internal morality," without which it is simply not law.[54] Suppose King Rex wants to establish a legal order. He will soon realize that he must use "rules" that have a certain degree of generality; he can't simply use ad hoc pronouncements. His edicts have to be public or they can't be followed. They can't be mere private thoughts. They have to be prospective, not retroactive. They have to be understandable. They have to be coherent and not contradictory. Citizens have to be able to comply with them. They can't be changed too frequently. They have to be minimally congruent with official behavior. If King Rex doesn't follow these principles, he won't just create a "bad" legal system—he will not create a legal system at all. These features are inherent aspects of "law."

Let us take these claims at face value: law isn't law without these features. How does this connect law and morals? Fuller claims that these features are inherent conditions of excellence in a legal order.[55] They are what make us cherish the "rule of law." They make human interaction "better." So law has an inherent "inner morality."[56]

I have never seen the force of this argument. Suppose King Rex wants to create a cheeseburger. He identifies seven ingredients: a bun, cooked ground beef, Swiss cheese, mayonnaise, onion, pickles, and ketchup. He even uses molecular content and weights to specify these ingredients. He seems to have described a cheeseburger with certain "essential elements," and he has not referred to a normative principle like "goodness." But now he notes that these components turn out to taste good and have nutritional value. Does that mean that we can't even *identify* a cheeseburger without reference to morals? I doubt that Bentham, Austin, Kelsen, or H. L. A. Hart were claiming that law is not a good way to organize human interaction. Kelsen, after all, said that law had to be "effective." And Hart affirmed that law must be at its core a system of mutual forbearances, enforced through coercion, that provides protections for individuals and their property.[57] Those are good attributes.

Next, Fuller argues that these inherent features of law—generality, publicity, and so on—increase the *likelihood* that lawmakers will promulgate "good" laws.[58] Nazi officials were aided in their efforts by often (but not always) acting in secret and in an ad hoc manner. Of course, even laws that follow Fuller's requirements can be evil. Elaborate slave codes satisfied all or most of them. But these features at least *help* make the content of law better.

Fuller's point here seems plausible. It is one reason we have sunshine laws and pay so much attention to process in our legal system. But, again, this is an empirical connection between law and morals, not an analytical one. There is no particular reason for a positivist to deny it. H. L. A. Hart, for example, could still "identify" this kind of law without referring to morals.

Fuller also challenges H. L. A. Hart's Rule of Recognition.[59] Recall that Hart says it is a *fact* in the world. But, Fuller argues, it would not be a fact if the legal system it identified did not create some minimally good order. Put another way, if the legal system it identified did not have some positive normative value, people would not "recognize it." So law and morals must connect, at least minimally.

Not to beat a dead horse, but once again Fuller's point, though plausible, is entirely empirical. It does not show an analytical connection between law and morals, which is the point positivists seem to deny. There might be several *empirical* connections between law and morals. The same human conditions that cause people to think murder is immoral are likely to cause them also to make murder illegal. Surely the positivists don't deny these empirical connections.

But Fuller has two arrows left in his quiver. They are connected, and both deal with interpretation and legal method. Both focus on the debate Fuller constructed about legal method among Keen, Handy, and Foster in "The Case of the Speluncean Explorers." And both rely on strands of twentieth-century linguistic philosophy, particularly the later philosophy of Ludwig Wittgenstein.[60] These are the arguments about the connection between law and morals that had the most significant impact on late-twentieth-century (and on current) legal thinking. Nearly all students (and teachers) accept the rough positivist premise that just because something is legal does not mean that it is moral and vice versa. That is, they are largely positivists. And they are relatively indifferent about the details of the academic debate. But the debate about *legal method* rages on, even in the halls of the Senate during confirmation debates. It turns out that it is also a prong of the debate about positivism.

FULLER ARGUES THAT we can't know what a directive means unless we know its narrative context and the purposes it is designed to accomplish.[61] Suppose a city council ordinance bans "vehicles" from a park. H. L. A. Hart would say that edict is law, without any reference to morals, because it was enacted by the city council, which was empowered by the state constitution, and so on. Finally we would get to the Rule of Recognition (something like commitment to American constitutionalism).

Fuller, however, says that we have only identified some *words.* A full understanding of what the *law* requires depends on what these words mean. Do they ban baby carriages? Bicycles? A battle tank serving as a monument? We can answer only by knowing the ordinance's *purpose,* which is a normative (moral) issue. Was it designed to cut down on pollution? Or to make a safe place for children to play? Either purpose suggests that a baby carriage is not banned. Reducing pollution suggests bicycles are not banned, but safety for children suggests that they are. We can know what the law *is* only by knowing the *ends* it is trying to serve. So these normative ends, or goals, or purposes are actually part of what the law *is.* This was Foster's methodology in "The Case of the Speluncean Explorers."

Fuller's argument tracks a certain strand of twentieth-century philosophy of language. In the early part of the century, philosophers such as Bertrand Russell and Alfred North Whitehead tried to understand meaning formally and logically. In his early work in the *Tractatus,* Wittgenstein was part of that effort.[62] But later, in *Philosophical Investigations,* he adopted a different approach.[63] Language is a contextual activity engaged by humans with purposes. Thus, famously, when parents tell the babysitter to teach their child a game, "game" doesn't include sex games or war games. That is because of context and purpose. This is not the place to investigate all of twentieth-century philosophy of language, but it is important to note that Fuller was influenced by it.

Under Fuller's view, certain seeming dichotomies are not as sharp as we might have thought. Means and ends are intertwined. So are facts and values. Consider a simple contract. We can ask questions about what a contract is, how it is formed, what are its essential elements, and so on. When we teach contract law to students, doesn't it make sense to start with these questions, probably first by starting with how to form a contract? That is what most law students expect.

But generations of law students started with a different question: What happens when you breach a contract? What are the damages or remedies? What values and interests does a contract protect? Specifically, do we return the aggrieved party to as good a position as she was in before the contract? Or do we put her in as good a position as she would have been in had the contract been fulfilled? If she buys wheat for $100 that ends up being worth $150 on the delivery date, does she only get her $100 back (a reliance interest) or does she also get the $50 profit (an expectation interest)? The answer, it turns out, is the latter.[64]

Why start with this question? Because in Fuller's contracts casebook (and many others that followed) he began with this question.[65] Why? Because we can't understand what a contract *is* unless we know what it is trying to do, that is, unless you know its purpose. Recall that we can't know whether a bicycle is a vehicle unless we know the purpose of banning vehicles from the park in the first place. So we start a contracts course with the idea that the purpose of a contract in law is to protect *expectations.* Very few students (or faculty) know why contracts courses start with the question of damages. It is because of Fuller's argument against positivism. (Alas, having forgotten this point, many contracts courses now start with contract formation.)[66]

Just as we saw with Keen, Hand, and Foster, one's position on the relationship between law and morals is related to legal method. How do we glean meaning from legal material? That is the central issue about learning to think like a lawyer. It is the central question about legal education. Fuller's work, along with that of other scholars at Harvard Law School, spawned a school of thought in the mid-twentieth century called "Legal Process."[67] We will examine it later in its historical context. For now it is noteworthy that it was profoundly influenced by Fuller's technical arguments about positivism.

Fuller's views about positivism affected legal education in yet a broader way. If law's purposes are actually part of law itself, not separate from law as the positivists claim, shouldn't we be teaching these purposes in law school, not just in the interstices of other courses, but in a systematic way? Shouldn't economics, political theory, Kantian ethics, and other normative theories be part of the curriculum? After all, they are part of "law."

Law schools have for a long time had courses in related disciplines. Legal history is intrinsically interesting to lawyers. Courses in forensic or general psychology might help lawyers select juries or examine witnesses. But the new movement in the latter part of the twentieth century was not to teach related disciplines as handmaidens to legal practice; they were offered to understand the meaning of law itself. Fuller implicitly invited these normative debates into law schools *as part of law.* This was the very thing Austin was trying to prevent!

FULLER HAD A final argument to counter H. L. A. Hart's attempt to separate law and morals. Actually, it is the same argument we just examined, applied not just to an individual law but to the Rule of Recognition itself.[68]

Hart needed his Rule of Recognition to be a "fact" so he could identify a legal system without referring to moral principles. So far, we have said that the Rule of Recognition in the United States is *something like* a commitment to our Constitution. But what is it *exactly?* We need to specify it in more detail so it can do the work of including some institutions but not others. Different people might differ about this detail by arguing for a slightly different articulation of a Rule of Recognition to better match our practices. So which specific articulation is correct? Fuller says we can resolve this ambiguity only by asking *why* we have a legal system (and therefore a Rule of Recognition). This is just a more abstract version of trying to resolve the ambiguity about what counts as a "vehicle." So even to specify the Rule of Recognition—which is crucial to H. L. A. Hart's attempt to define law without reference to morals—we need to refer to the goals and normative purposes of our legal system. But that connects law and morals in just the way that H. L. A. Hart sought to avoid.

FULLER SEEMS TO successfully show that we can't entirely separate law and morals. But his position is hardly one of strong natural law. He would not claim, as would Blackstone or Dr. King, that a bad law is no law at all. Today we almost never encounter a law student who fails to see the difference between a statute being *legal* and it being *moral.* In that sense, we are all positivists now.

Instead, Fuller shows us that we can't separate law and morals quite as completely as H. L. A. Hart (or others) would have wanted. At best, Fuller seems to take an anti-positivist position, or what we might call a neo-natural law position. Purposes including moral purposes are part of law in that we need to refer to them to resolve ambiguities. But they fall short of negating any and all laws that contradict those morals.

The questions about positivism and the relationship between law and morals have been historically important for legal theorists. Those questions are part of a lawyer's heritage, but they are not so hotly debated in ordinary political circles. But the offshoot of these issues—Fuller's claim that law and morals are connected because we need to refer to purpose to ascertain meaning—brings us back to a question that is at the center of political debate: How should (or can) judges faithfully "apply" the law rather than "make" it? That question, after all, goes to the heart of the very idea of "the rule of law." The technical debate about positivism had a major influence on it.

FIVE

HISTORICAL SCHOOLS OF THOUGHT: THE AMERICAN REVOLUTION TO WORLD WAR II

SO FAR WE HAVE EXAMINED some building blocks that might be used to construct overall ways of thinking about law. Law might be more or less formal, defer more or less to central authority, or be more or less coercive. Courts might have different status vis-à-vis other governmental and social institutions like legislatures and markets. Law and morals might be separate, or they might overlap. We might see different methods to extract meaning from texts. Much detail surrounds each of these issues, and certain combinations fit together in what we might call "schools" of thought. Indeed, we saw three of these combinations in the views of Justices Keen, Foster, and Handy in "The Case of the Speluncean Explorers."

AS IT TURNS OUT, each justice roughly represents a school of thought in America: Legal Formalism (Keen), Instrumentalism or Legal Realism (Handy), and Legal Process School (Foster). These are sketches. In fact, actual judges or scholars exhibit a variety of nuances. Most judges exhibit a variety of methods or don't explicitly talk about their method at all. But when they do talk about "schools of thought," these three rise to the surface.

Conventional wisdom holds that different methodologies and schools of thought prevailed in different eras of American legal history. This history is part of our legal culture, so law students and lawyers should be familiar with it just as a matter of cultural heritage. In addition, we might actually learn something about how our legal system works by observing how legal reasoning changes in different contexts, including under different historical conditions.

WE HAVE TO BE careful about categorizing different historical periods, especially according to "conventional wisdom." The conventional wisdom comes partly from Karl Llewellyn's narrative in *The Common Law Tradition,* written in 1960,[1] and Grant Gilmore's *The Ages of American Law,* written in 1977.[2] Both of these works use scant and selective historical evidence and questionable methodology. In 1975, a student reported that her senior thesis tested this thesis empirically. She divided cases by decade and examined a sample of opinions. Were they like Keen, or Foster, or Handy? She found that the distribution did not vary with historical eras. Maybe we are not examining changes in how judges actually think but, rather, changes in how legal scholars or judicial elites view these issues. Or maybe she was wrong. But the fact remains: there was a perception among these elites that there have been distinct historical eras in which the prevailing approach to legal reasoning changes.

Serious legal historians, including Morton Horwitz,[3] Robert Gordon,[4] Robert Cover,[5] David Rabban,[6] and others have given much richer and more thorough accounts of actual American legal thought in various substantive areas and in various historical eras. But the conventional wisdom is not wholly wrong, and in any event it lingers as part of our cultural legal heritage. It was the background, even if it was somewhat erroneous, of some of the jurisprudential thinking that shaped law and legal education.

One of these schools of thought—the Legal Process School associated with Lon Fuller and Henry M. Hart at Harvard in the mid-twentieth century—was and continues to be influential. It had a significant impact on legal education. We have already examined Fuller, and we will return to him in detail in due course. But it is difficult to understand Fuller without understanding the view he was critiquing—Legal Realism of the early twentieth century. And it is difficult to understand Legal Realism without understanding its nemesis—Legal Formalism of the late nineteenth century, and so on into Instrumentalism of the early nineteenth century. This is true even if these movements were responding to cartoons of earlier eras shaped by the conventional wisdom.

Jurisprudential movements are not alone in this regard. It is difficult to understand any philosophical or intellectual movement without understanding the problems it had inherited from its predecessors. Take Plato. Why would he develop an abstract and metaphysically problematic theory of the forms? It makes more sense when we consider the intellectual problem Plato himself inherited. Heraclitus, or so Plato thought, claimed that the world was nothing but change,[7] famously saying that you can never step in the same stream twice; the water will be different. Parmenides, by contrast, thought that change was an illusion.[8] His position led to Zeno's paradox[9] that Achilles's arrow will never reach its target; it will always just go halfway, and then halfway, and so on. Faced with these opposing positions, Plato took a very commonsense approach. He observed both change and continuity *seem* to occur, so how can we make sense of that? Objects in the physical world change, but they also participate somehow in their forms, which do not change.[10] The point isn't that he is right. It is just that we can understand him better if we understand the problem he inherited. So, too, with the jurisprudential schools of thought we are examining. The Legal Process School responded to Legal Realism, which responded to Legal Formalism, which responded to Instrumentalism. And then Law and Economics responded to the Legal Process School, and Critical Legal Studies critiqued them both.

There are many ways to approach history. In *The German Ideology,* Karl Marx held that the intellectual structure of an era is the product of the material structure of production—that is, of economics.[11] Of course, a great deal has been written about Marx's theory of history.[12] Suffice it to say here that material conditions and ideology are mutually supportive. Prevailing ideologies are influenced by prevailing economic structures, but they can also affect and change those structures. In any event, we need not resolve that issue. It is just worth noting that there are interesting relationships between jurisprudential schools of thought and the material and economic conditions of their era. So with these caveats in mind, let us turn to a brief survey of these historical schools of thought.

AT THE TIME of the American Revolution, American courts applied English and colonial common law and English and colonial legislation. Blackstone had published his *Commentaries* in 1765.[13] He was predominantly a natural lawyer, so one role for courts was to use reason to ascertain what natural law required. Blackstone was not as widely available in the colonies as were Coke's *Institutes,*[14] which were published about a century before, but they, too, reflected a natural law perspective.

Even Blackstone's *Commentaries* reflected a bit of positivism, as we saw in chapter 4. Natural law might be silent about details, leaving to humans the task of filling in the lacuna with positive law. And America needed *written* (positive) federal and state constitutions.[15] Nevertheless, the basic approach was natural law and natural rights. Indeed, the Declaration of Independence said that certain natural rights were "unalienable." They persisted even after the social contract established civil society.

Because law rested on a set of immutable natural principles, it was relatively unchanging and formal. With respect to social institutions, Blackstone held that courts (indeed, everyone) were absolutely subservient to Parliament.[16] This view had been the predominant English view since the Glorious Revolution at the end of the seventeenth century, when Parliament dethroned James II. At the same time, courts were active when it came to contractual dealings of private individuals. True, *Slade's Case,*[17] which recognized purely executory contracts, had been decided in 1602. Before that, only partially completed contracts were enforceable.[18] If a seller delivered goods but was not paid, he could recover the purchase price. Or if the buyer paid but did not receive the goods, he could get the goods or at least get his money back. But an entirely executory contract—one in which neither party had performed—was not enforceable. By enforcing executory contracts, *Slade's Case* supported the idea of a market economy. But when it came to damages, courts took a more centralized and less laissez-faire approach. Instead of enforcing the contract price, they enforced a "fair" price.[19]

With respect to liability and property rights, courts tended to protect passive (landed) wealth. An active party who injured another person was, by and large, strictly liable to a passive person without proof of fault.[20] Water rights of riparian landowners were governed by the natural flow doctrine.[21] Passive parties could recover from active ones who diverted water for productive purposes, such as a mill. Of course, this is just a sketch.

THINGS CHANGED IN the early 1800s. Morton Horwitz gives us a wonderful account in *The Transformation of American Law*.[22] By roughly 1825, we start to see more instrumentalism, or what Llewellyn calls the "Grand Style" of jurisprudence.[23] We see more of a willingness to change old rules through instrumental reasoning that pursued policy goals designed to help the burgeoning proto-industrial and commercial economy. The economy needed new forms of business organizations and new commercial instruments. Capital formation required the pooling of assets into corporations. The commercial economy needed negotiable instruments. These required a willingness to change old forms and rules into new ones, which in turn required an instrumental style. Put simply, there were a lot of freezing errors.

Of course, concerns about formalism and predictability did not go away. Legal opinions are not uniformly instrumental. Courts still pay careful attention to the language of statutes and the meaning of precedents. The codification movement reflected the idea that judges should not be making law.[24] The

Charles River Bridge case[25] challenged Massachusetts's ability to grant a new bridge charter across the Charles River because it violated the vested interests of the owner of an earlier bridge. But there seemed to be an *increased* willingness to use instrumental reasoning to change rules in favor of new social and economic needs, that is, to correct freezing errors.

Swift v. Tyson[26] is an interesting case. The question was whether a bank could create a negotiable instrument, that is, a note where the defenses a debtor might have against the original creditor are lost if the creditor endorses the note to a subsequent holder in good faith. Rural states such as Kentucky did not like negotiable instruments. The debtors were usually local farmers, and the creditors were often out-of-state banks. Not surprisingly, banks in Boston and New York favored negotiable instruments. The case arose in federal court under jurisdiction based on the parties' diversities of (state) citizenships. The question was whether the federal court had to follow Kentucky's rule on negotiability or could instead create a federal commercial rule. The Supreme Court held that the federal courts could adopt their own rule. Winds of change were in the air.

Tort law changed from something close to strict liability to negligence. Consider a railroad whose sparks from the engine create a fire on adjacent land. Under strict liability, the railroad would be liable in every case. Under the emerging law of negligence, however, the railroad would be liable only if it failed to take reasonable precautions to prevent sparks from starting fires. That was an enormous shift of capital toward industrial productivity.[27]

Contract law developed the principle of caveat emptor[28] (let the buyer beware) and started to enforce the "contract price" rather than the "fair price."[29] All of this helped create an increasingly laissez-faire market.

THE LATE NINETEENTH CENTURY saw a resurgence of formalism, or what came to be called "mechanical jurisprudence."[30] This is not surprising. Many of the freezing errors we witnessed in the early part of the century had been resolved. By the latter part of the century, many economic concepts favorable to industry and commerce were in place. We had negotiable instruments[31] and emerging forms of corporate governance.[32] Personal injury cases were governed by negligence, not strict liability.[33] A plaintiff's own negligence totally barred her recovery.[34] Indeed, under the "fellow servant" rule, even the negligence of a coworker barred a worker's recovery.[35] Throughout the law, the substance of most legal rules had become more compatible with active, risk-taking, productive enterprises in the burgeoning industrial and commercial economy. We have to be careful to avoid too simplistic a model, but the direction of these changes seems clear. One of the significant drawbacks of formalism, freezing errors, had diminished by the latter part of the nineteenth century.

Robert Cover has argued that instrumentalism also fell into disrepute after the Fugitive Slave Cases and then the Civil War.[36] As we saw in chapter 2, Lemuel Shaw, Herman Melville's father-in-law, was a key instrumentalist judge in the early and middle part of the nineteenth century, but he got caught up in the Fugitive Slave Cases. At one point, federal authorities seized the state courthouse in Boston by encircling it with a chain, and Shaw had to duck under the chains to enter the courthouse to send the slave back. This did not sit well with the abolitionists. We might see this as an act of formalism. Keen might have said simply that the letter of the law requires that a fugitive slave be returned and that it is irrelevant what morality requires. But the Fugitive Slave Act itself was seen as a pragmatic compromise to hold the union together.[37] Thus, enforcing the Fugitive Slave Law was also an exercise in pragmatism and consequentialism. What we needed was strict adherence to the nonconsequentialist moral principles.

The early American colonies and states were known as commonwealths, meaning that we are all in this together. With that type of mentality, it is easier to trust decision makers to do the right thing. It is easier to let judges use a nonformal methodology. There is nothing so detrimental to a sense of commonwealth as a civil war. Our Civil War may thus have been another factor that pushed us toward a return to formalism.

In the late nineteenth century, business enterprises were doing quite well without help from the government. If anything, businesses wanted the government to protect gains that they consider "vested." They thought that government generally, and judges especially, should simply stay out of the game. Thus, judges should be subservient to legislatures, and they should be subservient to private ordering in the free market. In the early part of the nineteenth century, it had been necessary for proponents of economic and legal change to hitch their wagons to judicial stars. Those stars were then favorable to economic development. But new stars rose and kept rising in the latter part of the nineteenth century. Charles Dickens was writing about squalid conditions in London.[38] Marx was writing *The Civil War in France*[39] about the Paris Commune. No need to have judges looking for new stars to hitch their wagons to.

Indeed, there was a danger that *legislatures* would hitch their wagons to these new stars. Late in the century, we see union activity and legislatures passing worker protection laws.[40] A thoroughly passive court would not be able to stop this. So we begin to see courts relying on constitutional provisions, primarily the Contract Clause and substantive due process, so they can curtail legislatures and protect vested economic rights.[41] But this was done with a formal style. Judges just "read" the Constitution to find that it mandated these results.

This suggests a very rough model for understanding changes in judicial methodology. The advantages and disadvantages of formality vary in different areas and eras. The substance of law in any particular era captures the economic and social needs of the era, but so, too, does legal philosophy. When social and economic conditions change rapidly, freezing and mapping errors become acute. Instrumentalism makes it easier for judges to alleviate those errors. When the need for change is over, formality and predictability can reassert themselves.

THE LATE NINETEENTH CENTURY also saw a rising belief that the law should be modeled on science.[42] Charles Darwin had published *The Origin of Species,* which expanded the reach of science. If scientific principles could be applied to the human condition, then why not to the law? And if law could be modeled on science, then it might protect judges from claims that they were inappropriately making policy choices reserved to the legislature. Applying scientific principles would supposedly be value neutral. Law as science might restore the prestige of the judiciary.

Law as science also fit with the emergence of German-style research universities in America. Beginning with Harvard and throughout the seventeenth century, American universities were typically theological finishing schools for the sons of prominent families. Later, they broadened their scope to become liberal arts finishing schools. They were not centers of serious organized research, particularly in science. German universities, by contrast, were. Slowly, major American universities began to adopt the German model.[43] We still have a dichotomy between major research universities and liberal arts colleges.

Moreover, universities started to engage in legal education.[44] Previously, lawyers learned their craft by "reading law" in the chambers of an experienced lawyer. Harvard Law School was the first, led by Justice Joseph Story. Then, later in the century, Christopher Columbus Langdell became dean and introduced to legal education the famous case method, which he combined with the Socratic method.[45] This was a seminal development in the history of legal education. The combination of the two methods is designed to teach students how to think like lawyers as much as to teach a particular set of legal rules. But Langdell also had in mind that the case method made the study of law more like science. Just as data observed in a laboratory formed the basis of scientific laws, cases could form the basis from which lawyers could develop general legal principles. By looking more like a scientific inquiry, law became a more respectable academic enterprise in the new American research university. Law no longer was merely a set of normative conclusions; it was a "scientific" analysis of "data." While we no longer think of this process as being scientific, the Langdellian methodology of legal education is still familiar.

Legal terminology also took on a scientific flavor. Consider the problem of proximate cause in tort law. A driver who negligently hits a pedestrian is liable to the pedestrian for her injuries. But suppose that, due to her injuries, the pedestrian stays home rather than going on an out-of-town trip. At a party, she meets someone, falls in love, and then gets married. Two years later, she visits her in-laws in another city, where she is murdered. Is the original driver liable for that too? But for the negligent driver, the pedestrian would not have been at the party and therefore would not have been at her in-laws. So the driver's original negligence was in fact a cause of the pedestrian's being murdered. Nonetheless, the negligent driver would not be liable to the pedestrian's survivors because he was not the *proximate* cause of the murder.[46] The murder was too far removed from the original negligence. The causal links between the two events were too attenuated.

There are good policy reasons that favor or disfavor liability under these circumstances.[47] The cases can get quite complicated. Historically, different jurisdictions have taken different approaches. But instead of analyzing policy, many courts couched the analysis in terms of the "links" in the "chain of causation."[48] Were there "breaks" in this chain? That rubric looks more scientific than normative. That was the rhetoric of law as science.

THE PENDULUM SWUNG back in the early twentieth century. The Progressive political movement started to produce social legislation, particularly surrounding the workplace.[49]

The Supreme Court regularly struck down this legislation as violating either the Contract Clause of the Constitution or the constitutional concept of "substantive due process."[50] Nothing in the explicit language of the Constitution prohibits laws that regulate working conditions, but the Court still found that those laws improperly interfered with the individual rights of workers and employers. Progressives objected that the justices were imposing their own political values on the cases camouflaged by claims that they are just "enforcing" the Constitution.[51] So the methodology of legal formalism and the rhetoric of law as science began to come under attack.

The watershed moment was Justice Oliver Wendell Holmes's dissent in *Lochner* in 1905.[52] The New York legislature had passed legislation limiting the number of hours a baker could work. The employers argued that this violated substantive due process. The Supreme Court agreed and struck down the statute. Justice Holmes dissented. One strand of his opinion relied on positivism, that is, the claim that law and morals are and should be rigorously separated. The majority, he claimed, was simply reading its own moral views about a free-market economy into a vague and indeterminate concept like substantive due process.[53] Holmes had advocated for positivism elsewhere when he announced his "bad man" theory of contract law.[54] Don't ask whether a contract obligates a party to fulfill it. That would inject moral considerations into the inquiry. Instead, just ask what will happen if a party does not fulfill a contract; they will be required to pay damages. So their legal obligation is simply to do one or the other.

For our current purposes, however, the second strand of Holmes's opinion is more important. The majority's claim of formalism was a façade[55]—and a pernicious one at that. Law is indeterminate. One reason is that it uses ambiguous language. What, exactly, does "due process" mean? It could mean specific substantive rights granted by legislation, or it might include implicit background rights embedded in our culture. There is no neutral way of choosing. "General propositions do not decide concrete cases."[56] Holmes also thought the majority's conception was too individualistic. More generally, the claims of formalism, that we can understand what law means apart from normative judgments and that law is like science, are just a façade.

There are other iconic examples. What if a statute simply directs the executor of a will to distribute the testator's assets to the beneficiaries named in the will, but the person whom the will names as the chief beneficiary, the testator's grandson, murdered his grandfather and did so to secure his inheritance?[57] Formalism says that the grandson can recover, but that seems to be an absurd result. Or consider an ordinance that bans "vehicles" from a park. Is a baby carriage a vehicle? Is a bicycle? Across the board, law's indeterminacy belies any claim of formalism.

In the area of common law, there are often conflicting lines of precedents. Should we limit them to their narrow facts? Or should we read them more broadly to encompass a general principle? There is no neutral answer to this question. We can't just say a precedent is limited to its narrowest facts, but surely a precedent applies more broadly than to plaintiffs wearing red shirts or to accidents that happen at ten thirty in the morning. For Holmes and other Legal Realists, judicial discretion in determining the law in these cases is inevitable.

Moreover, formalism is pernicious. It creates freezing errors that lock us in the past. The Progressive political movement reflected changing social values about workplace regulation. In 1880, a laissez-faire regime outlawing workplace regulation might have been acceptable. But by the time we get to *Lochner,* forbidding social regulation is discordant with the ethos of intellectual elites.

Legal Realism proceeded roughly in two phases. The first, sometimes called "Sociological Jurisprudence" and associated with Roscoe Pound at Harvard,[58] belonged to the period's Progressive political movement. It was not cynical but, instead, believed in the possibility of human progress. Law was a tool to effectuate that progress. Sociological Jurisprudence was first and foremost anti-*Lochner.* It was opposed to using the

Contract Clause and substantive due process to strike down social legislation. But it also embraced positions on other issues. It opposed a variety of doctrines in tort law that made it difficult for an injured plaintiff to recover, such as contributory negligence as an absolute bar to a plaintiff's recovery[59] and the "fellow servant" rule[60] that attributed a coworker's negligence to the injured party. It opposed as well the doctrine of proximate causation[61] that we discussed earlier. It too was often used to defeat recovery. Even though a defendant's negligence caused the plaintiff's injury, the causal links supposedly were too attenuated. Under the rubric of law as science, which purported to examine "links" in the causal chain,[62] this was often done without openly recognizing that it involved a choice of policy. There were doctrines in contract law that precluded consumers from recovering. In these ways and many more, the content of law was out of keeping with the Progressives' set of political values. There were lots of freezing errors.

THE SECOND PHASE of this movement was Legal Realism in full bloom, which took place mainly after World War I. We often overlook just how formative World War I was in affecting the intellectual outlook of the West. War is always horrific, but World War I was especially senseless. Stalemates in the trenches caused horrendous suffering. The machine gun made old tactics futile. And it was not altogether clear what the purpose of the war was. It was difficult after World War I to believe very strongly in the ideas of human reason and progress.

The heirs of Roscoe Pound were more cynical. They focused less on law as a tool for human progress and more on their belief that law camouflaged judges imposing their own political values on society. Formalism was a façade. By exercising their political values under the guise of formal legal rules, judges were usurping the role of the legislature. They were profoundly undemocratic.[63]

The later Legal Realists remained staunchly anti-*Lochner.* When the conservative justices on the Supreme Court continued to overturn progressive social legislation, these Realists continued to point out that the justices were just implementing their own political values.[64] They came to be called the "nine old men."[65] This issue came to a head under the presidency of Franklin Roosevelt. In the 1930s, Roosevelt and Congress adopted a great deal of social legislation. The nine old men continued to stand in the way, and Roosevelt threatened to expand the Court so that he could appoint a friendlier majority. According to popular belief, the nine old men got the message and began to change their tune. Thus, we had "the switch in time that saved nine."[66] Evidence of how some of the justices voted in cases the Court decided early in the New Deal, however, suggests that the switch was already in the making before Roosevelt proposed expanding the Court.[67] In any case, in the end, Holmes's dissent in *Lochner* prevailed.

KARL LLEWELLYN AND Jerome Frank were the leading figures in this later phase of Legal Realism. Frank wrote *Law and the Modern Mind* in 1930.[68] It introduced psychology to legal scholarship and legal education. If legal rules are not determinative to decide cases, then what is? A judge's thought process must be important. *Law and the Modern Mind* was important in its own right, but it was also important in fostering interdisciplinary work in legal education. We see the effects of this later in the twentieth century.

Llewellyn's books *The Common Law Tradition*[69] and *The Bramble Bush*[70] were enormously influential. Llewellyn was also enormously influential in substantive law. Contract law, under the influence of Samuel Williston in the late nineteenth century, was conceptual and formal.[71] Llewellyn was part of an effort to reform it through the Uniform Law Commission and the Uniform Commercial Code, to be adopted by the states. Somewhat ironically, the Uniform Commercial Code borrowed from formalism the idea that we need uniformity and thereby predictability in commercial law. But the content of the Uniform Commercial Code was much more flexible and realistic, reflecting actual commercial practices rather than abstract general principles. Llewellyn was the principal author of Article 2 of the code, which dealt with the sale of goods. It provided that a court should refer to industry practice,[72] trade usage,[73] and prior dealing between the parties[74] to interpret contractual obligations. So while Legal Realism is often characterized as being nihilistic and cynical, its actual participants were, by and large, lawyers in the end. For Llewellyn, at least, laws and legal language could make a difference.

THERE WERE OTHER indications of this as well. The Legal Realists were staunch supporters of Roosevelt's New Deal. Many of them worked in the administrative agencies he created.[75] They weren't socialists. Their solution to labor issues used market forces through collective bargaining.[76] Llewellyn focused on contracts in the private market. But neither were they advocates of laissez-faire economics. They understood that market imperfections often produce injustice so we need regulation. They would not enforce "unconscionable" contracts or contracts with wide disparities of bargaining power.[77]

So it is unfair to paint the Legal Realists as being nihilistic or as thinking that law has no meaning at all. But they did emphasize the ambiguities in legal rules and recognized that judges do make political judgments when they decide cases. The Legal Realists invite us to look behind the curtain in *The Wizard of Oz.* When we do, we see that there is just a human being behind the legal system, not a wizard. The Legal Realists, in other words, did much to demystify legal analysis. As a result, they invited the criticism that they were skeptics who thought that law and language had no meaning at all. Although that is a canard, it does cast light on how Legal Realism was received by some segments of the legal community.

THREE CASES CAPTURED the fancy of Legal Realists and became iconic centerpieces of twentieth-century legal education. The first was *MacPherson v. Buick Motor Co.*,[78] which we highlighted in chapter 3 to illuminate freezing errors. And as we also noted, it became the focal point of introductory teaching materials at Columbia Law School. They included a string of cases involving the liability of a manufacturer for a product defect, culminating in *MacPherson.* Recall from our earlier discussion that Buick manufactured an automobile with a defective wheel and sold it to a wholesaler, who then sold it to a dealer. The dealer sold it to Mr. MacPherson. When Mrs. MacPherson was driving the car, the spoke broke, and she was injured. She sued Buick, claiming it was negligent for not discovering the defect in the wheel.

Buick defended by arguing that the company was not in "privity of contract" with Mrs. MacPherson. Even though her claim was not based in contract, the rule in New York in a claim for negligence was that a product seller was liable only to someone with whom they had a direct contract. This is a surprising rule in negligence. In an ordinary case where a driver hits a pedestrian, the driver would be liable even though there was no contract. Nevertheless, the New York rule was well established for a product seller.

The rule dated back to an old case, *Winterbottom v. Wright.*[79] There the defendant had negligently repaired a stagecoach, but an injured passenger could not recover because he did not have a contract with the repairman. The New York Court of Appeals then made an exception when a pharmacist sold a poison mislabeled as a drug because it was *inherently* dangerous.[80] Poison is dangerous even if it is handled with care. Then the court applied this exception to seemingly more benign products, first to scaffolding used at a building site[81] and then to a coffee urn.[82] Finally, in *MacPherson,* Justice Cardozo held that the "inherently dangerous product" exception applied whenever a product is dangerous if defectively made. Of course, that result is contrary to the original holding in *Winterbottom v. Wright.* Surely a stagecoach is dangerous if defectively made. Moreover, even though Justice Cardozo continued to frame this as being an exception to the privity rule, the new holding actually swallowed the rule entirely: in any case in which a plaintiff is actually injured by a defective product, the product will be dangerous if defectively made.

So within the course of half a century, incremental decision-making had actually changed the rule.

Why are these materials appropriate to introduce first-year students to legal thinking? They fit Legal Realism. Law is not formal and static. It is flexible and instrumental. Good judges—and Cardozo was a great judge—can use legal material creatively to reach just results. Conversely, it dispels a formalistic approach to law. It reveals a man, not a wizard, behind the curtain.

MacPherson also highlights one of the most serious problems with formalism. The facts of *MacPherson* present an acute freezing error. When *Winterbottom v. Wright* was decided, most commerce took place face-to-face. For the automobile industry in the 1920s, however, the market had changed dramatically. Less commerce was face-to-face. Manufacturers increasingly used distribution systems employing wholesalers and retailers. Family members purchased products for use by other family members. In an economic sense, there *was* a contract between the manufacturer and Mrs. MacPherson. First-year law students who encounter this line of cases as an introduction to legal reasoning see formalism at its worst, with a grotesque freezing error. Fortunately, Justice Cardozo came to the heroic rescue. The subtext of these introductory materials is that the nine old men were mistaken. Just as Langdell's introduction of the case method at Harvard in the 1880s reflected the jurisprudence of formalism and law as science, the introductory materials at Columbia unmistakably reflected Legal Realism.

JUSTICE CARDOZO'S DECISION in *Palsgraf v. Long Island Railroad Co.*[83] was another watershed. It became a leading case in nearly every tort casebook. It addressed an important issue about the scope of liability for negligent conduct, but its importance transcended its doctrinal holding.

Mrs. Palsgraf was a "charwoman" who was taking her children to the beach. She was waiting for her train on the station platform when another passenger tried to get on another train as it was leaving the station. The train attendants tried to help him, but he fell, causing a package of fireworks he was carrying to fall and explode. The explosion knocked over a scale near Mrs. Palsgraf, injuring her. The jury found that the railroad was negligent toward the passenger trying to get on the train. The issue was whether the railroad's liability extended to Mrs. Palsgraf. Cardozo held that it did not because it was unforeseeable that the railroad's negligence to the first passenger would injure someone at the other end of the platform.

This is an interesting problem. Suppose a parent leaves a loaded gun on a table at a children's birthday party. That would be negligent because a child might be shot. But what if a child just dropped the gun on his foot? The parent was negligent, and "but for that negligence" the injury would not have occurred. But what happened to the child is not the reason we thought the parent was negligent in the first place. Some of the leading torts scholars of the era, including Leon Green, Learned Hand, Francis Bohlen, and Cardozo discussed the issue hypothetically.[84] A plausible case can be made either way.

Early English cases held that there was liability if a defendant's negligence directly caused injury, even if the injury is not the foreseeable harm that made us think that the defendant's conduct was negligent in the first place.[85] Later, the English courts reversed their position and held that liability extended only to foreseeable types of injuries.[86] At the time *Palsgraf* was decided, New York seemed to follow the earlier English rule.[87] So how did Justice Cardozo justify his decision?

In a dazzling display of fancy footwork, Cardozo reasoned that the question of *what* happened to a plaintiff was a matter of "proximate cause." In that case, a defendant is liable for unforeseeable injuries as long as they are "direct." "The law of causation, remote or proximate, is thus foreign to the case before us."[88] *Who* was injured is a different issue. That is a matter of "duty," and only foreseeable plaintiffs can recover.

Why should *what* happened and *who* it happened to be governed by different standards? Cardozo never says. Leo Lipson once commented that reading a Cardozo opinion is a bit like using a thaumatrope.[89] A thaumatrope has a card that can be spun very fast. On one side there might be a picture of a horse and on the other a picture of a rider. Or one side might have a picture of a bird and the other side a picture of a cage. When you spin the card you get the impression of a rider on horse or of a bird in a cage. For Lipson, Cardozo marshalled all of the facts and all of the law and then spun the thaumatrope. What we ended up with was a bird on the back of a horse.[90]

So why was this case so famous when it was decided in 1927? Progressive academics favored expanding tort liability; Justice Cardozo restricted it. Legal Realists would favor an opinion discussing the policy consequences of one rule over the other; Justice Cardozo's opinion was conceptual. Like night follows the day, the result depended on the label of "duty" rather than "proximate cause." But "proximate cause," with its links in the chain of causation, had the flavor of legal formalism and law as science. Justice Cardozo rejected that rhetoric. Duty *sounds* like a normative issue. Judges can't just claim they are eschewing policy judgments when they use it, even though Cardozo himself was short on policy. Indeed, Judge William Andrews's dissent based on "proximate cause" was full of candid discussion about conflicting policies.[91] But "proximate causation" was a dirty word. By eschewing it, Cardozo took a slap at law as science and Legal Formalism. He took a slap at the nine old men. The rhetorical nomenclature, not the result, helped explain *Palsgraf*'s iconic place in the canon.

JUSTICE LOUIS BRANDEIS'S 1938 opinion in *Erie Railroad Co. v. Tompkins*[92] is a third iconic case. It addressed a straightforward doctrinal issue. Federal courts have jurisdiction over cases involving questions of federal law, but they also have jurisdiction over cases between citizens of different states, their so-called "diversity" jurisdiction.[93] If the case had been litigated in state court, it would have been governed by state law. But what happens when it is litigated in federal court?

One would think that the straightforward answer is that state law still applies. But as we saw earlier in *Swift v. Tyson*,[94] the United States Supreme Court held that federal law applies. Recall that *Swift* involved the enforceability of a negotiable instrument, and burgeoning commercial interests favored both negotiability and a uniform federal rule. *Swift* gave them both. *Erie* reversed *Swift*, holding that in a diversity case the federal court must apply the state rule.

The substantive question in *Erie* involved tort liability of a landowner to a trespasser. Normally, a landowner has very limited duties to a trespasser, but there is an exception for very frequent trespassers in a limited area.[95] The common situation was where a community uses a well-beaten path across railroad tracks. The question in *Erie* was whether this exception applied not only to lateral paths across the tracks but also to longitudinal paths running parallel to the tracks. Pennsylvania state law said it did not. The federal district court, however, applied a federal rule that said it did and therefore favored the plaintiff. The Supreme Court overruled *Swift* and held that, in a diversity case, the district court must apply the state rule.

This is not an insignificant holding. It makes a big difference in actual litigation, where the plaintiff normally gets to choose where to sue. The old rule meant that the plaintiff could also sometimes choose the substantive law by choosing to sue in federal court. This is an important issue, but it is a relatively practical one.

Brandeis could have approached the case pragmatically. The old rule of *Swift* allowed forum shopping. He might have said that forum shopping was inconsistent with the Judiciary Act[96] that created the federal courts or with the Rules Enabling Act[97] that allowed them to develop procedural but not substantial rules. But Brandeis went further. He held that the rule in *Swift* was unconstitutional. Then he argued that *Swift* was unsound jurisprudentially. The problem was that the *Swift* court, rather than accept the fact that all law was the product of political sovereignty, seemed to think that there was a "transcendental body of law outside of any State but obligatory within it"[98] to be *discovered* by judges. *Swift* had a natural law flavor that was out of keeping with the positivism of Legal Realism.

But why did Justice Brandeis go to all of this trouble? What was bugging Brandeis? Why did *Erie* become a centerpiece for courses in civil procedure, much as *Palsgraf* had become the centerpiece for courses in torts? The "transcendental body of law" that Brandeis, following Holmes, complained about was a slap at the methodology of the nine old men and their ability to "find" substantive due process to overturn progressive social legislation. The specific result in *Erie* actually made it harder for an injured plaintiff to recover from the railroad. Not allowing injured plaintiffs to forum-shop also hindered recovery. These implications of his ruling seem to be out of step with a progressive agenda. But in Brandeis's hands, this relatively practical issue turned out to be the last nail in the coffin of the nine old men who purported to "find" legal principles in a "transcendental body of law" or the concept of substantive due process.

LEGAL REALISM THUS had an impact on the way courts and scholars analyzed legal issues. These iconic examples also indicate that it affected the canon of cases in legal education. *MacPherson, Palsgraf,* and *Erie* were an iconic triumvirate in first-year courses partly because they attacked the jurisprudential rhetoric of Legal Formalism and the movement to treat law as science. They supported Legal Realism and legal positivism.

AS WE APPROACHED the mid-twentieth century and the end of World War II, where did we stand with respect to Legal Realism? Its major tenets are that formalism is undesirable because it freezes us in the past, that formalism is a façade because legal norms are inherently ambiguous, and that law is a positivistic product of sovereign will. True, there are easy cases. H. L. A. Hart said these cases were in the "core." But "interesting" cases were in the "penumbra," where there are no clear or formalistic answers. In the penumbra, judges make policy decisions. If they claim to be deciding formalistically, they are fooling themselves and us. Of course, all of the important cases occur in the penumbra. So in all of them it is a mistake to think that the legal rules rather than a judge's values are the source of the decision.

Again, the judiciary and even the legal academy have never been monolithic about this viewpoint. Different judges and legal scholars held different views. But we can say that Legal Realism was a prevailing school of thought when we reached the mid-twentieth century. It had thoroughly discredited Legal Formalism, mechanical jurisprudence, law as science, and substantive due process. But at what cost? Didn't we still believe in the rule of law? Didn't law schools still teach doctrine? Was all of this just a façade, papering over the exercise of political power by judges? Judges are the pinnacle of the legal profession. Were they now relegated to being mere ciphers in H. L. A. Hart's "core" and unchecked policy makers in his "penumbra"? Was this democratic? Indeed, we still hear these criticisms of judges today. These were the issues that a new generation of legal theorists faced when America got back to work after the end of World War II.

SIX

HISTORICAL SCHOOLS OF THOUGHT: THE LEGAL PROCESS SCHOOL IN THE MID-TWENTIETH CENTURY

LEGAL REALISM PROVIDED an extremely effective attack on Legal Formalism, law as science, mechanical jurisprudence, and the nine old men. But it might also be seen as an attack on the very idea of the rule of law. It called into question the role of judges. Did they have a legitimate place in the American governmental scheme? By midcentury, judges were starting to do good things. They had outlawed school segregation in *Brown v. Board of Education*[1] in 1954, and they were reforming tort law[2] and contract law.[3] Maybe we should rethink Legal Realism. That is what Lon Fuller and Henry M. Hart at Harvard Law School thought.

Recall from his debate with H. L. A. Hart that Fuller thought law could not be entirely separated from morals. He was not a strong natural lawyer; a law could be immoral and still be a law. But he did think there were intrinsic connections between law and morals that could not be avoided. We surveyed these connections in chapter 4; one of them is relevant here. Interpreting law to ascertain what it means requires reference to its (moral) purposes. We can't know whether a rule that bans vehicles in the park includes baby buggies or bicycles unless we ask why it was passed. This opens the door for a judicial methodology that might answer the Legal Realists. We saw the outline for this methodology in Justice Foster's opinion in "The Case of the Speluncean Explorers."

For H. L. A. Hart, judges made policy choices in the penumbra. In this respect they were like legislators. That was the problem. If judges were merely acting like legislators, why would we need them? Maybe the answer is just convenience: we need someone to decide individual cases and adjudicate facts. We can't convene the legislature for every case. Yes, judges sometimes have to make policy, but that is just so they can adjudicate individual disputes.

But maybe judges don't even have to do that. True, legal norms have ambiguities. The Legal Realists were right about that. But judges have a methodology for resolving those ambiguities different from the methodology used by legislators to make policy. Judges can ascertain the purpose of ambiguous legislation (or common law precedents) and then apply it to resolve the ambiguity. Judges using this methodology are more than mere mechanical ciphers, but neither are they simply imposing their own political values on judicial results. They are applying the values of the legislature in a "thoughtful" way that enhances, not stifles, the legislative process.

So judges have a special methodology that is compatible with democracy. But they also have a special job because they decide special types of cases. Fuller distinguished between bipolar disputes—in which individual parties claim a legal right—and polycentric disputes—in which the legal outcome depends on balancing complex interests of diffuse social entities. Who was at fault in an automobile accident is an example of the former. What the appropriate tax rate should be is an example of the latter. Courts are not equipped to gather all the information necessary to resolve a polycentric dispute or to balance the competing social interests. But legislatures are not well equipped to resolve the specific facts necessary to decide who was at fault in an individual automobile accident. So we have a division of labor and of methodology between courts and legislatures. It is not true, as the Legal Realists claimed, that courts are just usurping the role of the legislature.

If courts should limit their "jurisdiction" to special kinds of cases and avoid resolving polycentric disputes, what doctrinal devices can they use? Article 3 of the United States Constitution provides that courts resolve "cases [or] controversies."[4] Which driver was at fault in an automobile accident is a controversy. What constitutes the appropriate tax rate is not. So we get doctrines like whether a person has "standing"[5] to sue, whether a case is "ripe"[6] for resolution, whether an issue is "moot,"[7] or whether it is a "political question."[8] These questions are a central part of a course in federal courts, which in the middle part of the twentieth century was as much about the philosophy of our court system as it was about practical rules for litigators. It is not surprising that Henry Hart taught federal courts and had the leading casebook.[9]

HENRY HART (ALONG with Albert Sacks) elaborated these ideas in seminal teaching materials called *The Legal Process.*[10] These materials were extraordinary. They were produced in 1954 as a set of mimeographed pages. They were lengthy (over 1,600 pages), unwieldy, and poorly edited. They were repetitive. Many of the topics had far too much reading for the classroom discussion they were intended to spawn. Nevertheless, as a whole they presented a vision of the American legal system and legal process that was deep, rich, and inspiring. Many professors in the late twentieth century took *The Legal Process* course in law school, which made the materials enormously influential. The Legal Process School helped invite other disciplines, such as law and economics, into the legal academy. Ultimately, it provoked a critique from a new group of legal scholars, which came to be called "Critical Legal Studies" and challenged the underpinnings of the Legal Process School as being reactionary and naïve. The impact of these materials was enormous.

A hallmark of *The Legal Process* materials was that they dealt almost entirely with run-of-the-mill cases. They began, for example, with a controversy about a shipment of cantaloupes that was delayed on a train and spoiled.[11] They dealt with a revenue-sharing lease for a five-and-dime store,[12] bills of lading,[13] and lost baggage under an airline tariff.[14] A few of the cases—such as the Steel Seizure Case[15] during the Korean War—were of historic note, but those cases were rare.

Using quotidian cases was a huge asset. Inquiries into a legal method today almost always involve cases of historic and political importance. We debate Justice Scalia's use of literalism or originalism in consequential constitutional cases. Or we examine the Supreme Court's reasoning in cases involving race, gender, sexual orientation, or abortion. These are important issues. As a consequence, subtle nuances about legal methodology get lost in larger political debates. Trying to focus on purely jurisprudential issues in consequential cases is difficult, especially in class discussion. It is like trying to compare subtleties of technique in paintings by Claude Monet and Édouard Manet by shining a searchlight on them. When the underlying substantive issue involves the meaning of a bill of lading, it is much easier to focus on the jurisprudential and methodological issues. We can learn more about legal method from easy cases then we can from hard ones.[16]

Although Fuller was not an author of *The Legal Process* materials, his influence is unmistakable. His insistence that we cannot separate what law is from what it is trying to achieve is the central methodological point. His insistence that courts are well equipped to handle certain types of disputes but not others is another central theme. We can sense his discussions with Henry Hart on almost every page.

THE LEGAL PROCESS materials begin with a long saga about "The Case of the Spoiled Cantaloupes."[17] The shipper sues the railroad for the damage, but the saga involves more actors than just the railroad and the shipper. The shipment takes place under a bill of lading, which in turn was agreed to under a tariff that had been approved by the Federal Trade Commission. The Federal Trade Commission had been authorized by Congress. The relationship of the actors is dynamic. Congress can amend the statute. The Federal Trade Commission can change its rules. The railroad can amend its tariff. The shipper can try to change the bill of lading.

What is the message? Surely it is not that we learn more about the law governing cantaloupe shipments. Hart and Sacks are presenting a picture of what constitutes law. Recall that Bentham, Austin, Kelsen, and H. L. A. Hart all had their own definitions of law. For Hart and Sacks, "law" is the output of the complex interactions of various "legal" players. Law is whatever this complex dance produces. We still have to know who counts as a "player," so Hart and Sacks do not give us a rigorous definition of what counts as law and what doesn't. But they do give us a different way to look at this issue. Law is what this complex set of interactions produces. It is the product of a legal "process."

This approach has a number of salient features. First, it focuses on the way we go about resolving disputes more than on substantive outcomes. Courses like federal courts, civil procedure, administrative law, and conflict of laws became central to legal education. Questions about how our legal system works are paramount. Even in a substantive course like labor law, the focus was on the process of collective bargaining and the procedural role of the National Labor Relations Board (NLRB).

Second, the system reached solutions through dialogue and interaction among the many players. It reflected intellectual modesty in which no single person or institution has a monopoly on truth. This resonates with the American government's structure of federalism and separation of powers. It may seem frustrating at times, but we muddle through to achieve adequately just results by trusting the system. The group, by hashing out its differences, can achieve better results than an individual or single institution. It favors compromise. How different from the sentiments of today!

Both of these features are reflective of Plato. In Book 1 of the *Republic,* Socrates asks, "What is justice?"[18] Several of the people at the gathering that is the dialogue's setting propose answers: justice is what benefits our friends and hurts our enemies;[19] justice is what favors the strongest;[20] and so on. Socrates then cross-examines them, in turn, to see whether their answers can withstand scrutiny. With each answer he determines that it cannot. Book 1 ends with no one having given a satisfactory answer to Socrates's question. Nor does Socrates tell us what justice is. Have we made no progress? Actually, we have. We may not know precisely what justice is at the end of Book 1, but the dialogue to this point has at least brought us closer by eliminating some of the possibilities.

Later, in Book 7, Plato gives us the allegory of the cave.[21] The inhabitants are shackled and can see only the wall of the cave in front of them. There they see shadows cast by a light and intervening objects behind them. Their only "reality" consists of the shadows on the wall; they are oblivious to the objects behind them. For Plato, this is an allegory for his belief that our own physical world consists of "shadows" of perfect forms that exist in another world. These forms constitute what is truly real; physical objects merely reflect it.

How can the prisoners (or we) come to understand more about the true reality? Plato does not tell us, but he does show us. If we engage in Socratic dialogue—reasoned speech, or *logos*—we can at least approach the truth. If we engage in the kind of reasoned dialogue that Socrates uses, we will make progress. Each of the actual participants in this Socratic dialogue is more enlightened at the end.

Hart and Sacks seem to agree. If we will let the institutional participants in our legal system have an ongoing "dialogue" over time, we will get better (not perfect) answers to legal questions. This is a deeply modest view of human progress.

Hart and Sacks are Platonic in another sense. For Plato, we obtain social justice by designing a just state.[22] Rather than try to describe the standard of justice directly and then judge whether the results of a dispute are just by that standard, Hart and Sacks attend to the structure of our legal process. If we get *that* right, we will be more likely to reach just results. Indeed, maybe that is the definition of a just result. This is like a lot of life in other areas. Don't worry about getting a hit at each at-bat in baseball, just focus on having a good at-bat. The results will come. Focus on the process, and the results will take care of themselves.

SO WHAT IS the role of *courts* in this system? Are they, like the Legal Realists claimed, just making policy and thereby usurping the role of the legislature? Or do they have a special role? One thing they do is oversee the entire system to make sure that everyone is doing her proper job. They are like the point guard in a basketball game. Their first task is to decide who should get the ball.

Consider *Jenkins v. Rose's 5-10-25¢ Stores.*[23] The landlord leased retail space to a five-and-dime store, with a percentage rent provision based on receipts. The five-and-dime did well and then moved to a new location for the remainder of the lease. Did the store owner still have to share the receipts? Was there an implicit provision in the rental agreement that the owner would stay put for the lease's term? A court's first task would be to identify the proper player in our legal system to answer that question. Is it for the legislature to decide what is fair? Or for the court? No. For Hart and Sacks, the proper place to resolve this question is for the parties themselves to decide in a market transaction.

Hart and Sacks were protecting their left flank, defending courts against the claim that they were interfering with market transactions. Hart and Sacks, like the Legal Realists, were politically progressive, and they did not believe in an entirely unfettered or laissez-faire marketplace. They believed in reasonable regulation. But they were not socialists. The first place for resolving a dispute about the terms of a lease would be "private ordering" in a free market transaction.

A twist on this, however, is that Hart and Sacks reveal a certain antimarket attitude when they call private market transactions "private lawmaking." It is as though the state somehow "delegated" the job to private individuals rather than treat the rights individuals exercise in market transactions as endowments they have inherently and not by some dispensation of the state. The market for Hart and Sacks is, one might say, as much an arena of "state action" as any other. Hart and Sacks may not be socialists, but they don't seem to be libertarians either.

In any event, the first task in a contracts case is to look at the contract itself. In the multiplayer legal system Hart and Sacks envision, "private ordering" has an important role. In other cases, we will see a court looking to other entities, such as the legislature, or an administrative agency, or a common law precedent. Making this decision is not the trivial task of a cipher. It is a "supervisory role" that requires a deep understanding of our legal culture. But neither is it simply policymaking that displaces the role of the legislature.

Now the court has another task. Did the proper player—here private ordering—actually do its job? The answer in *Jenkins v. Rose's* is no. The parties overlooked the possibility that the store owner might move. So at this point the court needs to fill the gap to give the contract meaning. But this is only because the institutional participants normally assigned this task—the parties—dropped the ball. The court is not disturbing the role of the private parties. It is helping them. And this could happen for any of the other primary institutions that constitute the players in our legal system.

With respect to the legislature, for example, consider *Riggs v. Palmer.*[24] A New York statute of wills directed the executor of the estate to distribute the property of the decedent to the beneficiaries named in the will in accordance with the decedent's instructions. It made no exception on account of a beneficiary's involvement in the decedent's death. In this case, the decedent's grandson, who stood to inherit the bulk of the estate, murdered him. The other beneficiaries, the decedent's daughters, brought suit to exclude the grandson from inheriting under the will, and the court ruled in their favor. The court, in ruling that the "Felonious Heir" should not be able to recover, was not taking over the role of the legislature. In deciding as it did, the court was not simply disagreeing with a judgment of the legislature that anyone named as a beneficiary in a will, even if he murdered the testator, is entitled to the portion of the estate that the will instructs the executor to transfer to him. The legislature, after all, could not possibly have considered this possibility. So there is sometimes a gap in legislation, and the court needs to help by filling it in.

We will examine later the *methodology* a court should use to fill in a gap when the primary decision-making institution failed to do its job. The point here is that the court's initial job—the "point guard" job—is first to decide which of the many institutions in our legal system has the authority to provide the substantive answer to the question of what legal action to take and then to decide whether this institution actually did its job.

Courts also sometimes have the role of being the primary source of decision. Sometimes no other legal institution has an answer. Take an automobile accident. The parties do not have an existing contract, there is no property rule or entitlement, and the legislature or administrative agencies might not have provided a rule of decision. But there has to be someone who can resolve the dispute. And if no other legal institution has done so, the court has the obligation to resolve the dispute by providing a common law norm.

Hart and Sacks fully embrace many aspects of Legal Realism. They agree that pure formalism is not possible because legal norms are riddled with ambiguities. As we have seen, sometimes the primary decision maker left a gap. Sometimes the language of a statute or contract is ambiguous, as in the word "vehicle" in an ordinance that bans vehicles from the park. Sometimes the common law has conflicting lines of cases. Hart and Sacks examine cases involving all of these ambiguities. *Jenkins* was one of them. Hart and Sacks try to answer the Legal Realists, but they agree with them that law can be ambiguous. Hart and Sacks are not formalists.

SO, IN *JENKINS* the court notes that there is an ambiguity in the lease because the parties have not addressed the issue of whether the store owner can move with impunity. So what should the court do? Send the parties away? Or try to ascertain what the parties actually meant, even though they didn't expressly address the issue? A court should do the latter because that is more faithful to the parties' purposes. The role of the court is to help the parties achieve what they were trying to do. Similarly, if this had been a statute—such as in *Riggs v. Palmer*—the court would be more faithful to the legislature by trying to ascertain what the legislature was trying to do. Hart and Sacks call this process "reasoned elaboration."

How would this work in *Jenkins?* The parties were trying to implement a certain type of economic deal. The store owner might have limited resources in a startup business and therefore could not afford a high fixed rent. But if the business succeeded, he would be able to pay more. The landlord was willing to take the risk of the business's failing in return for a greater payout if the business succeeded. The landlord was "buying" part of the future income stream in what effectively was a joint venture. It would be inconsistent with this "essence" or "purpose" of that deal to allow the store owner to back out when the store became successful.

The court is not acting as a mere cipher. The court's job of reasoned elaboration is a sophisticated and worthy one. But neither is the court trying to substitute its values for those of the parties. It is trying to further the goals of the parties. Suppose I tell my housekeeper to go to the market to get some soup meat for lunch. Has she violated my instructions if she goes in the store and buys soup meat but, knowing we don't have the other ingredients, buys them too?[25] Or would I be annoyed if she served just the meat for lunch and not the rest of the soup?

Later we will examine some problems Hart and Sacks might encounter with this approach. Some of these problems are bases for an overall critique of the Legal Process approach that influential scholars in the next generation mounted. The point here is to get an idea of the basic structure of Hart and Sacks's theory.

HART AND SACKS address a variety of cases to demonstrate how reasoned elaboration works. One involved the question of when a railroad's responsibilities to take care of shipped goods ends.[26] The railroad unloaded the goods onto the station platform and locked them behind a gate until the shipper could pick them up in the morning. They burned during the night. Had the railroad "delivered the goods," or was the railroad still responsible? There were two lines of common law precedents. One held that transport by buggy ends only when the goods are delivered to the door. Under that line of cases, the railroad would be responsible. But another line of cases held that a sea vessel completes its responsibilities when the goods are unloaded on the dock. That line would favor the railroad. Which line of precedents controls? In many ways, a railroad is more like a buggy. It has wheels and transports goods on the land. But given the purpose of the distinction, aren't trains more like seagoing vessels? Buggies can navigate the streets. They can actually get to the shipper's door. Seagoing vessels and trains can't.

This type of reasoning is like the game on *Sesame Street*: "Which of these things doesn't go with the others?" Suppose we have an umbrella, a swimsuit, galoshes, and a tuxedo. We could eliminate the umbrella because the others are pieces of clothing. Or we could eliminate the tuxedo because it doesn't involve water. Law students first learned reasoned elaboration on *Sesame Street*!

Consider a federal statute that requires railroads to have automatic couplers between the cars of its trains.[27] A worker was injured when he went between a car and a locomotive to couple them by hand. Both had automatic couplers, but one was a Miller coupler and the other was a Jenny coupler. They would couple automatically with their own type, but not with each other. The worker claimed that, because of this mismatch, the railroad had not complied with the statute.

The railroad argued that it had literally complied with the statute because the locomotive was not a car, and, in any event, they were equipped with "automatic couplers." The court of appeals agreed.[28] Hart and Sacks rejected this literal approach. The terms "car" and "automatic coupler" are ambiguous, but given the purpose of the statute—promoting job safety by relieving workers of the necessity of going between the cars to form a train—the statute meant to include the locomotive and to require couplers that work with each other. Ultimately, the Supreme Court agreed.[29]

A PROBLEM WITH literalism is that it is incompatible with the way language works. Hart and Sacks follow Wittgenstein's view of language.[30] Words alone don't convey meaning; words in context and in light of the purpose with which they are being used do. Hart and Sacks rely on a series of "jokes" to make the point: "Bartender [after receiving a live lobster from a tipsy customer as a gift]: 'Thank you very much. I'll take him home for dinner.' To which the customer replied, 'Oh don't do that. He's had his dinner. Take him to the movies.'"[31] In context, the meaning is clear. The literal interpretation is funny only because it is absurd. This suggests that Hart and Sacks seem to think that reasoned elaboration is not just a *better* method of interpretation from a policy perspective. They seem to think that it is inherently *correct* from the perspective of how language works. Legal Formalists aren't just wrong as a matter of policy or even how our legal system works. They are wrong from the deeply philosophical perspective of how language works.

IN ADDITION TO playing point guard and employing a special method, courts are special because they handle only certain types of cases. Courts are ill-equipped to handle other types of cases. Hart and Sacks follow Fuller on this point. Courts are good at handling bipolar disputes based on legal rights; they are not good at handling polycentric, forward-looking disputes based on balancing competing social interests and policies. For example, they should not decide political questions. An example in *The Legal Process* materials is the famous *Youngstown Steel Case*[32] decided during the Korean War. In response to labor strife in the steel industry, President Truman seized the steel mills. A strike would have disrupted the supply of steel needed for the war effort. For Hart and Sacks, this was a complex policy question that should not be decided by a court.

Hart and Sacks also relate an interesting vignette, "The Invitation to Dinner."[33] The invitee promised to attend, knowing that the host had gone to special trouble and had told the other guests that the invitee would attend. When he didn't show up, the host was extremely embarrassed. All of the formal elements of a contract were there, but Hart and Sacks think a court should not intervene. There are just some types of disputes courts should not handle.

WHAT HAPPENS WHEN a court tries to use reasoned elaboration to resolve an ambiguity but the purpose is itself ambiguous? Consider again the city ordinance that bans vehicles from the park. If the purpose of the ordinance was to reduce pollution in the park, a bicycle is not a vehicle. If it was to make the park safe for children to play, a bicycle probably is a vehicle. So far, so good. But what if it is unclear what the city council was trying to do? Or given that the city council consists of many people, maybe different people had different purposes. How should a court resolve that ambiguity? Maybe the purpose is clear. But maybe not.

We live our legal lives in the "shadow" of higher-level legal decisions. With the Supreme Court, there is a procedure "point" at the top of our legal structure. Hart and Sacks talk about the Great Pyramid of Legal Order.[34] Only a small fraction of legal disputes ever get into court, much less to the appellate courts or the Supreme Court. This is primarily a procedural point. But we might also have a Great Pyramid of Purposes. In theory, a court could continue climbing that pyramid for higher and higher purposes to resolve ambiguities in purposes lower down. If the pyramid comes to a point at the top, reasoned elaboration might ultimately get to the right answer.

To make this work, however, we need a legal culture that roughly agrees on its ultimate purposes. We need a culture that is sufficiently cohesive. For Hart and Sacks, the ultimate purpose at the top of the pyramid is roughly utilitarian. The ultimate goal of our legal system is to maximize our citizens' satisfaction of their needs and wants.[35] Hart and Sacks think that this is a relatively uncontroversial claim. At least they do not spend much time arguing for it. The important point is not what they think constitutes the apex of the pyramid. It is that they seem to believe there is one, that we have a relatively cohesive society of shared goals. We will return the question of whether this is a plausible view of society, either in the 1950s or today.[36]

RONALD DWORKIN IS arguably the most influential legal philosopher of the late twentieth century. First in a *Harvard Law Review* article "Hard Cases,"[37] and then in a series of books,[38] he made an argument similar to Hart and Sacks's. By looking deeply into our legal system's purposes, including our deep moral commitments, we can resolve ambiguities so as to ascertain a "right" answer, even in hard cases. Dworkin's legal philosophy is nuanced, and it evolved over the years. We will not capture it all here. But it is very similar to the idea of reasoned elaboration. The major difference is that Dworkin's background moral philosophy is based on moral rights rather than utilitarianism. Dworkin builds on the jurisprudential work of Hart and Sacks (and Fuller) and also on John Rawls's Kantian moral philosophy. One wishes he had given them more credit. For Dworkin, even our deepest moral theories are part of law. They and the specific cases they help to decide exert "gravitational force"[39] that influences how an answer to any new case is ascertained, even if the purely "legal" materials are ambiguous.

Whether or not Dworkin's method will work depends on whether our background moral theories are themselves susceptible to reasonably unambiguous interpretation. We will see in chapter 7 that they are not. For now the point is to understand how Hart and Sacks and Dworkin *thought* they were using our culture's background moral commitments to resolve ambiguities on the surface of legal norms and thereby answer the Legal Realists.

SO WHAT WERE the problems with Hart and Sacks? One was that they (and Dworkin) seem to think that the deeper we delve into our moral values, the more we agree. They think there is a point at the top of the pyramid. This might have been plausible in 1954. We had defended the world against fascism; we were aligned in an effort to move the country forward economically; we wanted to improve racial justice (at least in the circles that Hart and Sacks inhabited); and we were fighting communism. Of course, there were intramural political debates, such as around labor unions, but our deep goals had a fair amount of unity. But then came the Vietnam War. By the time we moved into the late 1960s and 1970s, it was hard to assert that, at the deepest levels, we all shared common goals.

A second problem was that Hart and Sacks say judges should use reasoned elaboration, but where are they standing when they say that? What are their criteria? Are they sociologists who are just describing our judicial system? Are they claiming that judges using reasoned elaboration will make the world better? Are they claiming that reasoned elaboration is the only philosophically plausible way to interpret language? On these questions they are silent. They don't tell us the criteria we should use to judge their own theory.

A third problem was Hart and Sacks's aversion to constitutional issues.[40] Judges had begun following a progressive agenda for criminal justice and other constitutional issues by ruling a number of statutes and practices unconstitutional. Even as early as 1954, the Supreme Court decided *Brown v. Board of Education*.[41] *Griswold v. Connecticut*[42] was decided in 1965 followed by *Roe v. Wade*[43] in 1973. But Hart and Sacks were dubious about ruling a statute unconstitutional. The Legal Process was just that: a process. It involved dialogue and adjustment among different legal institutions such as private ordering, legislatures, administrative agencies, and courts. Ruling an action or statute unconstitutional cut off that dialogue. *Brown* also had the disadvantage of being based on social science and social policy. That was the type of polycentric policy approach that was not appropriate for courts. So Hart and Sacks were skeptical of judicial review at a time when judicial review was popular among academic elites. Questioning *Brown*, for example, was not politically advantageous.

In addition, Hart and Sacks, for all of their opposition to formalism, needed formalism to make their system work. Consider three examples. Recall the case of the automatic railroad couplers. A literal interpretation of the statute was inappropriate because words alone don't have meaning. One must also look to purposes and context. The purpose of the statute was to promote worker safety. But suppose a railroad worker fell off the top of a freight car that did not have a railing. Would he be entitled to recover under the automatic coupler statute? After all, the purpose of the statute was worker safety. Why should it matter that the statute did not mention railings? The percentage-revenue lease in *Jenkins v. Rose's* never mentioned the possibility of the store owner's moving, but the court read it into the lease. So why not read other dangers into the railroad statute? Hart and Sacks actually analyze a number of cases to distinguish between expanding language and contracting it. But the point is that, even aside from purpose and context, words do seem to have limits as to what they can mean. The automatic coupler statute simply did not apply to railings. But, then, why not just stop with the words before getting into purposes in the first place? Why is that anymore arbitrary than invoking the purpose of worker safety to expand the statute beyond couplers?

Hart and Sacks also seem to depend on a one-rule, one-purpose fallacy. In the automatic coupler statute, it is likely that the legislature was balancing competing purposes, such as worker safety and the cost of running a railroad. When it came to automatic couplers on cars, the balance favored safety. But would it be worth creating a monopoly for one type of automatic coupler? That *might* have tipped the balance the other way. We just don't know. How can you extrapolate from a compromise? The same is true for a contract. Maybe the landlord in *Jenkins* was willing to gamble that the store owner wouldn't move?

Why use reasoned elaboration at all? Or what does reasoned elaboration mean? It certainly means the judge should not send the parties away in *Jenkins* simply because the contract did not mention the possibility of moving. The court should instead engage in reasoned elaboration. But why? One reason might be that this method of judging will better promote the goals of our legal system. It will help individuals maximize the satisfaction of their wants and desires. But what if, as an empirical matter, telling judges to act literally would aid predictability and thereby facilitate those goals better than reasoned elaboration? In that case, wouldn't Hart and Sacks favor literalism? But they never consider that. They seem to apply reasoned elaboration come hell or high water. Isn't that formalism?

Consider a court's role as the point guard. What if the court determined that the NLRB was the appropriate decision maker and that the agency had done its job? But what if the particular decision was horrendous? Wouldn't it frustrate the purpose of deferring to the agency—maximizing the satisfaction of human wants and desires—to defer in this case? Hart and Sacks seem to defer no matter what, because that is the court's "job." Isn't that a formalism that Hart and Sacks are trying to critique? But if the court looked to this ultimate purpose, wouldn't it be doing precisely what the agency had been charged by the legislature to do? That is precisely what the Legal Realists claimed.

Finally, isn't it easy for a judge to "cheat"? Can't she find a purpose that suits her political views? Can she conclude from the wrongheadedness of a result that the primary decision maker must not have done its job? Justice Keen made this very point.

SO THERE ARE several problems with *The Legal Process* materials even on their face. But that is likely to be true of any powerful, rich, and interesting account of our legal system. Hart and Sacks still provide very powerful answers to some of the questions raised by the Legal Realists. True, courts sometimes seem to act as though they are making policy, and if they're not careful they sometimes seem to be acting like legislators. This is due largely to the ambiguity of legal norms.

Hart and Sacks agree fully. But *many* of these ambiguities can be resolved by appealing to context and purpose. If nothing else, Hart and Sacks describe a methodology that can dramatically reduce the size of H. L. A. Hart's penumbra. And courts are forced into resolving these ambiguities because they have other roles to play. Legislatures are not good at resolving bipolar disputes between individual parties that depend on factual claims. And someone has to play the role of point guard to make sure that different institutions and our legal system are doing their job. The fact that there are some loose ends may be unduly harsh criticism.

In any event, Hart and Sacks's methodology of reasonable elaboration became a staple of legal education. It is a staple of legal reasoning even today. Courts should pay attention to the kind of case they are trying to resolve. Courts are good at some things but not others. This is a cautionary tale in today's world where courts are often asked to address extremely complex social problems.

Hart and Sacks were influential (as was Dworkin) in setting the ground rules for legal education. If legal ambiguities can be resolved by looking to background normative and moral theories, and if those background normative and moral theories are actually part of law, shouldn't they be studied in law school? In the late twentieth century, we witnessed an influx of law professors grounded in cognate normative disciplines, such as law and economics and various strands of moral and political theory. And the agenda is now set for a generation of legal scholars whose critique of the Legal Process School constitutes the Critical Legal Studies movement. We will return to all of this in due course.

First, however, we need to take a detour to examine the types of moral theory that might help us resolve the ambiguities we find on the surface of our legal norms. Do any of them do this job effectively? If any of them did, then the critique of the Legal Process School that constitutes the Critical Legal Studies movement would have little force. Critical Legal Studies would, instead, be merely an opposing school of thought. Its place relative to the other schools would merely correspond to a new justice on the Supreme Court of Newgarth whose jurisprudential view rivaled the views of Justices Keen, Handy, and Foster. So the import of the Critical Legal Studies movement depends on the outcome of an examination of the different moral theories that could back up the interpretive method of the Legal Process School. And, as it turns out, these moral theories are additionally interesting because they address law's political and moral legitimacy and our moral obligation to obey it.

SEVEN

TWO BACKGROUND MORAL THEORIES

WE HAVE BEEN tracing a historical timeline of jurisprudential theories about how judges decide cases. We will return to that timeline when we investigate how Critical Legal Studies responds to the Legal Process School. But we will not be able to fully appreciate why the Legal Process School was vulnerable to the Critical Legal Studies' criticisms unless we understand and evaluate the role of moral values in the School's method of resolving ambiguities in legal norms atop the Great Pyramid of Legal Purposes. And to understand and appreciate the role requires an appreciation of the two moral theories, one or the other, of which Legal Process scholars ultimately needed to back up their method of reasoned elaboration. These theories stand in the background of the Legal Process School's program.

Moral theories are interesting for many reasons. They are what we use (often implicitly) to critique individual behavior or social arrangements, including the content of our legal norms. Presumably, legislators are motivated by moral or normative principles when they enact laws. Even the staunchest positivist recognizes that.

Some moral questions are more intimately related to the structure of law itself. One such question is: What method should judges use? We might find a "legal" answer to this question, such as the plain meaning rule in contract and legislative interpretation, but we might also answer it from a moral perspective. Like any other social practice, the reasoning of judges can be analyzed and critiqued morally, and there is a variety of moral theories that can serve as bases for this endeavor.

We might also ask whether it is moral for the state to impose a legal system at all. What morally justifies a legal system's coercion of people? Or from the perspective of an individual, do we have a basic moral obligation to obey the law? Does the fact that an edict is law add to our moral obligations? These are moral questions, not legal questions, but they implicate the nature of law, not just its content.

The Legal Process School highlights how moral theory is relevant to law in yet another way. For Fuller, Hart and Sacks, and Dworkin, what law means in ambiguous cases is ascertainable only by referring to the moral values it is trying to further. These moral values are thus no longer separate from law; they are part of law. Even "purely" legal arguments sometimes make reference to these background moral values. As moral theory becomes part of law itself, it appropriately becomes part of the law school curriculum. A first-year law student who is asked whether a particular law is fair is not being asked merely an interesting question of social ethics. She is being asked to identify the moral underpinnings of a particular law so that she can use those underlying purposes to interpret and apply the law to other settings.

This method supposedly answers the challenge of the Legal Realists that law is hopelessly ambiguous and that judges impose their own political values when deciding cases rather than "following" the law. The moral values a judge uses to ascertain what the law means are not the moral values of the judge; they are the moral purposes of the legislature or earlier courts. So courts are "passive." But to succeed in answering the Legal Realists' challenge requires a background moral theory that is sufficiently determinate. We can ascertain whether it actually is only by looking at how various moral theories work.

So we have three areas of inquiry for a moral theory. What does it say about the state's moral right to coerce citizens? What does it say about an individual citizen's moral obligation to obey the law? And is it capable of performing the task given to it by Legal Process scholars of answering the Legal Realists by resolving ambiguities in legal norms?

THERE ARE SEVERAL texts we might look to for moral theories. A religious text like the Ten Commandments or the Book of Leviticus sets out a system of rules that mandate certain moral behavior. *The Iliad* and *The Odyssey* present a picture of human behavior that might be taken as a moral theory, as do Confucius's *Analects* and the Tao. But rather than extract a moral theory from such texts, we should look directly to two prominent moral theories in the Western tradition that have dominated the analysis of moral issues presented by our legal system. They are *utilitarianism* and *social contract theory.*

First, some general points about moral theory itself. A moral theory normally focuses on two objects of study. The first is the appropriate goals of human activity, or what moral philosophers call "the good."[1] Should humans pursue material wealth, beauty, friendship and love, the glorification of God, and so on? The second is the rules or principles of right and wrong that constrain how we might go about pursuing the good. This is what moral philosophers call "the right."[2] It is useful to identify a moral theory's conceptions of the *good* and the *right.*

Second, it is useful to understand how a moral theory's conception of the right is related to its conception of the good. Some moral theories evaluate whether an act is right by asking whether it increases or decreases the good. These are generally called "consequentialist" theories. Acts are right if their consequences promote the good. Rules of right and wrong are instruments for producing good results. Other moral theories, often called "deontological" theories, determine whether an act is right or wrong according to criteria that include some that do not depend on its consequences for promoting or diminishing the good. Utilitarianism is a consequentialist theory. The social contract theories we will examine are deontological.

UTILITARIANISM IS ASSOCIATED mainly with the English philosophers Jeremy Bentham[3] and John Stuart Mill.[4] Utilitarianism holds that an act is morally right to the extent that it maximizes human happiness. It identifies the good with human happiness.[5] Thus it identifies the right with maximizing the good. That is why it is a consequentialist theory. It is the poster child of consequentialist theories and is sometimes mistakenly thought to be the only consequentialist theory. Actually, it is possible to have a consequentialist theory that identifies the good with something other than human happiness. We might identify the good with the glorification of God and then ascertain whether an act is right simply by asking whether it maximizes, or even increases, the glorification of God. Or we might identify the good with aesthetic beauty and then identify the right with maximizing beauty. Nevertheless, utilitarianism is by far the most widely accepted modern form of consequentialism.

Much literature evaluates the strengths and weaknesses of utilitarianism.[6] There is an intramural debate within utilitarianism itself about what human happiness consists of.[7] Does it consist of maximizing the satisfaction of human choices—something like a market theory—or does it consist of maximizing a certain feeling of euphoria in the brain? This difference is critical for understanding issues surrounding the work of John Stuart Mill. In his essay *Utilitarianism*,[8] he argues that right action is action that maximizes human happiness. But in *On Liberty*,[9] he argues that the state cannot interfere with self-regarding conduct. This latter edict seems to be deontological, not consequentialist. What if state interference with individual liberty actually promotes human happiness? The answer may be that Mill defines human happiness as the satisfaction of human choices.[10] If he had defined happiness as a neurological state of the human brain, the two parts of his work might not be compatible.[11]

Another intramural debate is how we can make interpersonal comparisons of happiness.[12] How do we know that one person does not experience happiness or agony more intensely than another? And why focus narrowly on humans? Why not include all sentient beings, including higher animals? Or why include all humans? Why not just focus on the happiness of our tribe or political entity? Are we trying to maximize aggregate happiness or average happiness? Is happiness like temperature, or is it like heat? A small object like a cup of tea might have a high temperature but not much heat. A large object, like an ocean, might have low temperature but more heat. The difference would have an impact on our policies that affect the size of the population.

What is the time horizon for maximizing happiness?[13] If it is a millennium, we might adopt policies that forgo early consumption so that we can increase consumption later. If it is a generation, we might prefer consuming more early on. There is nothing objectively "correct" about the right time frame. It makes sense for individuals to maximize over an expected lifetime, but that assumes that we do not value the happiness of future generations.

How a particular moral question comes out in utilitarianism depends on these issues. Until they are answered, utilitarianism is radically indeterminate, in addition to being hopelessly fuzzy and dependent on empirical questions. So it does not seem to do the work the Legal Process scholars had in mind: resolving ambiguities in legal norms by looking even deeper into our moral values.

THESE ARE CONCEPTUAL problems. Utilitarianism also has normative problems because it fails to provide a good account of some of our strongly held intuitive moral judgments. Most of us consider slavery to be morally wrong *regardless of its consequences.* A utilitarian could argue that slavery does not maximize human happiness. Whatever "benefit" it provides to slave owners is surely offset by the detriment to slaves. But most of us think that a moral condemnation of slavery should not have to depend on that empirical point. Slavery is just wrong, without any regard to a balancing of its consequences.

Philosophers like to use a pair of hypotheticals to make this point. Both hypotheticals involve a driverless, runaway trolley barreling down a track toward five men who are working on the track and unaware of the oncoming trolley.[14] In one hypothetical, there is a bystander who happens to be located next to a switch that can divert the trolley onto a spur where there is another worker who is also unaware of the runaway trolley. By pulling the switch and diverting the trolley onto the spur, the bystander can save the five workers on whom the trolley is bearing down, though the worker on the spur will be killed. In the second hypothetical, there are two bystanders standing on a footbridge above the track watching the trolley race toward the five workers. One of these bystander's is a large man who, if he fell in front of the trolley would stop it from killing the five, though his being run over by the trolley would be fatal. The other bystander can therefore save the five by pushing this large man off the bridge so that he falls in front of the trolley. In either hypothetical, then, a bystander can save the five endangered workers by taking an action that kills someone else, so the consequences of the action are the same in either case. What seems clear, however, is that the morality of the action is not the same.

A utilitarian, to the contrary, would hold that the moral permissibility of the bystander's action is the same in either case. Killing one to save five is for a utilitarian the right action to take. Yet intuitively only in the first case is the action arguably permissible since the death in this case is a side effect of pulling the switch to divert the trolley onto the spur. In the second case, the action taken by the bystander is morally wrong, for intuitively it is immoral to purposely kill one individual as a means to saving five others. A utilitarian might simply respond that it is a mistake to think there is a moral difference in the bystander's actions in the two cases. But the point here is not to resolve this particular dispute in moral philosophy; rather it is to point out a perceived weakness of utilitarianism or, for that matter, any consequentialist theory. Our intuitions seem to suggest that sometimes there is more to whether an action is right or wrong than to the goodness or badness of its consequences.

Another normative problem with utilitarianism is that it is relentlessly and excessively demanding. It is always "on." It judges us at every moment, and at every moment we fail.[15] Even as I am writing these words, and as you are reading them, we are failing to act morally. Surely there is something we could be doing right now that would increase aggregate happiness more than writing and reading. We could be giving blood or earning more money to send to refugees of war. The next thousand dollars in my bank account surely would do more good in the hands of the Red Cross than for whatever I will spend it on. Utilitarianism gives us a good admonition that we often could use our own resources more effectively if we weren't so "selfish." But do we really think we are being "immoral" if we aren't altruistic at every moment? Is it always "immoral" to favor spending money on my family rather than on refugees from a war-torn country? The point is not to resolve these moral issues; it is that utilitarianism does not provide any safe harbor for purely individual choices. Individuals can never simply favor their own interests instead of maximizing aggregate happiness.

Maybe we do maximize aggregate human happiness by giving people "rights" that insulate them from the immediate dictates of utility. Our practice of "property rights" that we can use as we please might itself contribute in the long run to utility by incentivizing people to work hard and invest. Sometimes this approach is called "rule utilitarianism."[16] The idea is that maximizing human happiness justifies the rule, but the rule adjudicates individual cases. This is just a different moral theory from true utilitarianism (act utilitarianism). But maybe the rule's contribution to happiness is just an empirical fact under act utilitarianism. An actor would, at each moment, have to judge whether the contribution to happiness of the individual act was outweighed by the act's impact on undermining the system of rights. This formulation would still require a utility calculation at every moment, although accounting for the effect of the rule would now be part of the calculation. It might provide some relief for having the liberty to prefer one's own interests, but it would still be exhausting.

Notwithstanding some concerns, utilitarianism does have a certain commonsense appeal. We often see utilitarian arguments in daily discourse, especially when we are talking about issues of broad social policy. What should our policy be about taxation? Let us try to figure out what tax rate would make the best contribution to our aggregate welfare. True, that doesn't exhaust our moral concerns. Some people would be more concerned about inequalities in the tax system, or infringements that taxes might have on individual liberty in the market. But it would be hard to claim that utilitarian arguments are not pervasive on issues of this sort.

IN ANY EVENT, we have enough background on utilitarianism to address the questions that legal theory might pose to a moral theory. The first is whether the state is morally justified in coercing its citizens through law. For a utilitarian, the answer seems to be relatively unproblematic. Of course coercion impinges on individual liberty, but this is not a problem for utilitarianism. A utilitarian isn't interested in promoting liberty for its own sake; she is just interested in maximizing human happiness. Liberty might itself contribute to human happiness, but that is simply an empirical question. As long as our system of laws itself maximizes happiness, a utilitarian would be satisfied.

This takes us back to chapter 3. Law is a centralized, coercive, formal system. These features have benefits such as increasing predictability, allowing decisions on complicated issues to be made centrally by experts, and so on. At the same time, a centralized, coercive, formal system has drawbacks such as mapping errors, freezing errors, alienation, and so on. If we add up all of these positive and negative effects, we can decide whether law contributes to happiness.

If the question is whether we should have *any* legal system, utilitarianism has an easy case. At the end it is an empirical question, but it seems obvious that we are better off in terms of aggregate human happiness by having at least some legal regulation. As Hobbes famously said, without law life would be "solitary, poor, nasty, brutish, and short."[17]

But for a utilitarian, answering whether to have some legal system at all would not end the inquiry. The features we noted in chapter 3 come in degrees. We can have more of them or fewer of them. We can have a legal system that is more central or less central, more formal or less formal, more coercive or less coercive. We can have law intrude on more aspects of our lives, or we can have it intrude on fewer. All of that goes to the structure of our legal norms. We could also have judges act more like Keen, Handy, or Foster. For a utilitarian there would be optimal levels of these features, at least in theory. As we leave a state of total anarchy, the positive aspects of having "more" law would be very high and the negative aspects would be low. As we acquire more law, however, the added marginal value of even more law would decrease and the marginal negative value would presumably increase. There is no easy or even feasible way to know precisely where this happens, so this model is a metaphor as much as it is an analytical fact. The point is that a utilitarian would think that having some law will increase human happiness but that it is also possible to have too much law.

Moreover, the positive and negative aspects of law might be felt differently in different areas. In areas of commercial interaction, predictability might be important, whereas the dangers of alienating human interaction might be small. In areas of criminal law or child welfare, however, it might be just the opposite. We may want more centrality in regulating securities markets but less centrality in regulating the bedroom. We may want more flexible standards for ascertaining child custody but more formal rules in tax law. Indeed, that is the kind of mixture our current legal system actually has.

In the end, a utilitarian would answer all of these questions by trying to ascertain the mixture that would maximize human happiness. The answer would be vague, but the types of arguments would be clear. And surely the answer would not be to forego a legal system altogether.

OUR SECOND QUESTION is the flipside of the first: Even if the state is morally justified in imposing a legal system, what are the moral obligations of individuals to obey it? Do individuals have any moral obligation to obey the law? Individuals sometimes have a moral obligation that coincidentally requires them to do what the law would require them to do. A utilitarian would think that it is immoral to gratuitously kill another person. Coincidentally, or even because of that moral judgment, the law also makes murder illegal. The question is whether the mere fact that an act is illegal ipso facto means that individuals have a moral obligation to refrain from engaging in it.

There are three possible answers to this question.[18] One is that it makes no difference at all to one's moral obligations that an act is also illegal. Under this approach, law would be transparent to our moral obligations.[19] We would look straight through law to the ultimate standard of morality to ascertain our moral obligations. Being transparent, the fact that the conduct was also illegal would not have any effect on our moral obligations. A second possibility is that there is an absolute moral obligation to obey the law. Under this approach, law would be opaque.[20] If we know that we have a legal obligation to do some act, then we need look no further to ascertain whether we have a moral obligation to do that act. The third possibility is that the fact that law addressed the conduct makes a difference, but not a conclusive difference, to our moral obligations. Law would be translucent.[21] We would look to our ultimate moral standards through law, and the presence of law would *affect* our view. It would not totally *block* our view of our ultimate moral guideposts.

For a utilitarian, it seems quite clear that law would be translucent with respect to our moral obligations. As we saw earlier, the mere fact that we organize our affairs through a legal system contributes to overall happiness in complicated ways. It increases overall happiness by increasing predictability and allowing us to plan our affairs, but it sometimes detracts from overall happiness with mapping errors and freezing errors. If a utilitarian would say, on balance, that having a legal system roughly at the level we do creates more aggregate happiness than no legal system at all, then she would take this fact into account in deciding her ultimate moral obligation in a particular case. She would first ask about the consequences of her action in terms of aggregate happiness in the individual case. Then she would take into account any impact her obedience or disobedience might have on other people obeying the law. If she runs red lights, will other people run red lights, thereby making it harder to rely on traffic laws? She might also take into account the fact that the rule had already been decided by people more expert and knowledgeable than herself. She might also take into account the cautionary observation that she might have biases compared to the entity that promulgated the legal rule. In short, a utilitarian would weigh all the pros and cons—in terms of happiness—of a particular act and then add to them the impact her obedience or disobedience would have on the conduct of others and thereby on the rule of law.[22] The mere fact that law prohibited the conduct would tend to support a moral obligation to obey, but this impact could be outweighed by the negative consequences of the conduct itself.

The situation is actually more complicated. A utilitarian might think we live in a society with too much law. Or she might think that we live in a society where blind obedience to law is too pervasive. In that case, setting an example of disobedience might actually have a positive impact. Thus, the mere fact that specific conduct is outlawed would be a reason for *disobeying*. In short, a utilitarian would note that law in and of itself has an impact on human happiness and that individual decisions to obey or disobey can have an impact on the efficacy of that system. This, in turn, would be part of a utilitarian's calculus in evaluating a particular course of conduct. But it would not be conclusive.

A DISCUSSION ABOUT our moral obligation to obey the law often includes a discussion of civil disobedience. Especially in the nineteenth and twentieth centuries, civil disobedience was a powerful form of political protest. Henry David Thoreau famously discussed it in his essay "Civil Disobedience,"[23] and it played an important role in the political movements of Gandhi, the antiwar protesters of the 1960s, and the civil rights activists, especially Dr. Martin Luther King Jr. There are many versions, but the classical one is that it is morally appropriate to disobey the law to protest its immorality as long as one does it openly, peacefully, and for reasons of conscience.[24] The protester must also be willing to accept the punishment. The use of civil disobedience in the second half of the twentieth century in America was complicated by the fact that the protesters often claimed that the laws they were disobeying were not only immoral but also illegal because they were unconstitutional. The protesters often were not willing to accept the punishment, but that was because the conduct was not even illegal. Some antiwar protesters fled to Canada to avoid punishment. Suffice it to say that civil disobedience comes in many forms.

Civil disobedience fits nicely into a utilitarian framework, even if the protesters themselves do not rely on utilitarianism. Instead, they might rely on pacifism, equality, self-determination, or anti-imperialism. The issue is how a utilitarian would evaluate disobedience. It might be an effective utilitarian strategy to refuse to obey a particular law but nevertheless to minimize the negative impact of the disobedience on the overall system of law. If the "contagion effect" of disobedience can be limited to certain ritualized events—where the disobedience is public, open, peaceful, for reasons of conscience, and where the protester will accept punishment—the protester might be able to maximize the effect of her specific conduct while minimizing any negative impact disobedience has on the overall rule of law. A peaceful sit-in to protest an unjust war while accepting the consequences of punishment is unlikely to have much impact on the propensity of other individuals to follow traffic laws or pay their taxes.

The answers to all of these questions might be hopelessly vague, but the *structure* of a utilitarian analysis is relatively straightforward. It may not answer the questions exactly, but it at least provides a coherent structure for debate. A utilitarian analysis of these questions takes on the intuitively familiar structure of balancing pros and cons of a particular course of action. Whatever shortcomings utilitarianism might have from a philosophical point of view, it at least rings true to the style of much political discourse.

OUR HISTORICAL SURVEY of American jurisprudential schools leaves us with a third question. For the Legal Process School, a background theory is supposed to be able to resolve ambiguities in legal norms, thereby countering the Legal Realists' claim that judges resolve these ambiguities by referring to their own political and moral preferences. For Fuller and Hart and Sacks—though not for Dworkin—the background moral theory seems to be something like utilitarianism. The goal of our legal system is to maximize the satisfaction of people's preferences. The question is whether utilitarianism can perform the task Fuller and Hart and Sacks assigned to moral theory. If the meaning of a statute or even its purposes are ambiguous, can utilitarianism resolve the ambiguities?

It appears that utilitarianism is hopelessly unable to perform that task. Even at first blush, the question of whether a particular interpretation will increase or decrease aggregate human happiness is hopelessly dependent upon empirical questions with indeterminate answers. Some questions might be easy. We might agree that abolishing our highway system would decrease aggregate human happiness. But most of the questions we face—such as whether to build a *particular* highway—almost always provoke plausible arguments on either side. And the lack of a clear right answer will be even more prevalent as we probe deeper and deeper into our moral values for answers to our most troublesome legal and social questions.

Utilitarianism is even more fundamentally indeterminate in ways we discussed earlier. Exactly what counts as human happiness? Economists might try to solve this technical problem by using dollar equivalents as a measure,[25] but even today we have the entire realm of behavioral economics that challenges classical economics.[26] And even if we can agree on a measure of human happiness, we still have the problem of defining the time horizon over which we are trying to maximize it.

Even if we can transcend all of these problems, we are left with a methodology of balancing the pros and cons of a particular decision. Isn't that precisely the policy-oriented methodology used by legislators? Didn't the Legal Process School claim that courts don't just act like legislators? So we haven't made much progress answering the Legal Realists. Didn't Fuller say that these are polycentric problems that courts are not well-equipped to resolve? Fuller was trying to demonstrate that courts have a special role and methodology in our governmental structure. Utilitarianism looks like the balancing of policies we expect in legislatures.

So let us take stock. By insisting that our background moral commitments are actually part of our legal system because they are part of our interpretive methodology, the Legal Process School invites our attention to questions of moral theory to resolve ambiguities. Utilitarianism does provide insights about our legal system and our moral obligations toward it, but for the task of bringing closure to ambiguities in legal norms, it is a weak candidate.

THE OTHER PREVAILING moral theory in the late twentieth century is a deontological theory that emphasizes rights irrespective of their consequences. It is a version of political and moral theories that rely on the idea of a social contract. The theory Dworkin favors for resolving ambiguities in legal norms is a version of these theories. The idea of a social contract in modern philosophy can be traced back at least to Thomas Hobbes[27] and John Locke,[28] but we will be examining the later theories of Jean-Jacques Rousseau, Immanuel Kant, and John Rawls.

How can the state justify coercing individuals given our commitment to individual liberty or freedom? If we believe in the divine right of kings, it is easy to justify the state. If God rules the universe and appoints kings to rule on earth, it follows that the king's edicts are morally justified. But when we stop believing in the divine right of kings, what gives the state the moral authority to coerce people?

Social contract theory borrows a commonsense idea from everyday life. How do individuals in everyday life exercise their own freedom to bind themselves? They enter into contracts. So why not use this idea metaphorically to explain why collectively we are bound to obey the law? In an ordinary contract, we bind ourselves because we receive a quid pro quo. What is the analog in a metaphorical contract to explain our political obligations? For Hobbes, it was getting peace and security. He thought that life in the state of nature—that is, without law—would necessarily and fairly quickly degenerate into a war in which everyone was each other's enemy.[29] It would be, in his memorable expression, a war of all against all.[30] Individuals would have unrestrained liberty, but they would be in constant danger of being killed. They would gladly give up some of their natural liberty for the peace and security that the state and legal system could provide. For Locke, the quid pro quo was not only getting peace and security in our relations with others but also protecting our natural property rights.[31]

These arguments are pragmatic and straightforward. Just as a utilitarian would say that we will be "happier" in a civil society with a legal order, so Hobbes and Locke argue that individuals are "better off" in a civil society. The only difference is that, for Hobbes, individuals are "better off" because they can live in peace and be protected from the dangers of war, whereas for Locke individuals are "better off" because they have greater protection in the enjoyment of their property. And by making this argument within the metaphor of a "contract," Hobbes and Locke overcome the objection that the state's use of coercion to maintain order is an attack on individual liberty. Individuals in a state of nature would *freely* give up a portion of their liberties to obtain these protections. Hobbes and Locke offer interesting political theories. But they do not offer deep moral theories. Rousseau does.

ROUSSEAU FAMOUSLY STARTS *The Social Contract*[32] by saying: "Man is born free, and everywhere he is in chains. . . . How did this change come about? I cannot tell you. What can make it legitimate? That question I think I can answer."[33] Rousseau does not argue for abolishing the state. He is not in favor of absolute freedom in a state of nature. Rather, he argues for the form a state must take to be legitimate. Rousseau laments the corrupt condition of society, but he does not think we can ever return to a state of nature. The process of civilization is irreversible. Instead, he thinks we should attend to the institutions that shape our character in modern society: our families, our education, and the state. We need to reform these institutions so they produce individuals and a society that exhibit admirable qualities. He addressed the family in *Heloise.*[34] He addressed education in *Emile.*[35] He addressed the state in *The Social Contract.* Rousseau's approach resonates with Plato's argument in *The Republic* and with Hart and Sacks's approach in *The Legal Process.* If we are interested in individual justice, we should attend to the structure of the state (and other institutions that affect us). We will focus on the state and *The Social Contract.*

In Rousseau's social contract theory, a legitimate state is one whose citizens enjoy civil liberty that is equivalent to the natural freedom they give up in forming a state. To form a state in which every citizen enjoys civil liberty that is equivalent to the natural freedom each possessed in the state of nature requires investing the lawmaking power of the state in the people themselves. The form a state must then take to be legitimate is that of a pure or direct democracy, a state in which the supreme legislature consists of all of the people and in which the votes of the members of this legislature count equally. Only in a direct democracy can each citizen's obedience to the laws represent obedience to himself as the maker of those laws, and this is the condition of a state's legitimacy. The reason, Rousseau argues, is that only in a direct democracy can a man continue as a self-governing agent when he exchange life in a state of nature for life under the laws of a civil society. Only then is each citizen his own master and not the slave of another.

Rousseau's version of the social contract by which a legitimate state is formed is thus different from Locke's (and Jefferson's) version. In Locke's version, individuals, by retaining some of their "unalienable" natural rights, exchange a portion of their natural freedom for greater security in their enjoyment of the remainder.[36] As Rousseau sees things, individuals in Locke's version are still in a state of nature. In Rousseau's version, an individual must give up all of his "natural rights" to leave the state of nature and realize the civil liberty that comes with living according to laws that he gives to himself. Rousseau calls such liberty "moral freedom."[37] His social contract is an exchange of natural freedom for moral freedom.

ROUSSEAU'S DISTINCTION BETWEEN natural freedom and moral freedom is a consequence of his idea that the passage from a state of nature to a civil society transforms human beings from creatures governed solely by their instincts to creatures capable of being governed by reason.[38] Once a population of human beings comes together as a sovereign people, each member of the population acquires the capacity for rational deliberation about the general good of the community they now constitute. And when these deliberations yield legislation aimed at promoting the general good, the resulting laws express the will of the people, or what Rousseau calls "the general will."[39] Indeed, Rousseau holds that the enactments of the legislature are laws only if they represent exercises of public reason and express the general will.[40] Otherwise, they merely represent the sum of the influences of different individual biases, inclinations, and passions within the population and not the conclusions of public reason. Obedience to directives that are merely the outcome of toting up votes cast without regard to the general good of the community cannot be understood as obeying oneself. It is not a realization of moral freedom.

After the social contract, sovereignty rests with the people, not with the government.[41] The social contract does not form a government at all. The sovereign people in civil society create a government to administer the laws they enact, and they can suspend it whenever they want.[42] The government the people create in civil society can take a variety of forms. It could be a monarchy, or an oligarchy, or a democracy.[43] But in none of these is the government the repository of sovereignty; sovereignty remains with the people.

The people as sovereign make laws according to majority rule. If the votes they give when legislating reflect rational deliberation aimed at promoting the community's good, then the legislation is an exercise of public reason and its outcome is a declaration of the general will. In this sense, the majority is the arbiter of the general will. Modern sociological theories about politics and voting blocs suggest that the connection between majority rule and reason is tenuous. And Rousseau is not blind to the weakness in this connection. His distinguishing the general will from the sum total of individual biases, inclinations, and passions reflects his awareness of how easily a democratic assembly can abandon reason. Voting that does not follow deliberation about the best means to promoting the community's good is not an exercise of public reason. It lacks the underlying agreement on ultimate ends that gives unity to the deliberative process, and accordingly Rousseau recognizes how factions and private interests can destroy the general will. An important part of his program are the measures he recommends as needed to mitigate the economic and demographic factors that encourage such factions and strengthen the motives of private interests.

HOW DOES ROUSSEAU'S theory of the social contract help answer our three questions about our legal system? First, for any state that meets the conditions of legitimacy that the theory sets out, it gives a straightforward justification for that state's use of coercion through a legal system. That is the whole point of the social contract. A legal system coerces people in a way that seems to be inconsistent with their liberty. But the citizens of a legitimate state have given up their natural liberty by forming civil society; they have gained in return civil liberty by virtue of being collectively the authors of the laws to which they are subject. [44] This is not inconsistent with liberty; it is an exercise of liberty. In being subject to laws that express the general will, they are obeying only themselves and are thus as self-governing as they were in the state of nature. Of course, if a state fails to meet the theory's conditions of legitimacy, then its use of coercion through a legal system is unjustified. That so few states have ever met these conditions explains Rousseau's opening statement: that, while men were born free, they are everywhere in chains.

Second, the theory also gives individuals who live under the laws of a legitimate state a straightforward answer to the question of whether they have moral obligations to obey those laws. As long as the laws are the result of exercises of public reason and express the general will, there is an absolute obligation for an individual to obey them. If, however, they merely represent the sum of the influences of different individual biases, inclinations, and passions within the citizenry, an individual has no obligation to obey them. So unlike utilitarianism, which had an extremely vague and conceptually nuanced answer to an individual's moral obligation to obey the law, Rousseau's version of the social contract seems to provide an all-or-nothing answer. It is either radically obligatory or radically revolutionary.

HOW DOES ROUSSEAU'S version of the social contract perform as a background moral theory to resolve ambiguities in our legal norms? It does not provide much help. The general will does not itself have any intrinsic normative content. All we know is that it is whatever the majority says it is. Does that mean that, every time there is a question about an ambiguity in a legal norm, we simply look to the majority to resolve it? Would we ask a judge to predict what the majority would say? We could, but that would be an unsatisfactory answer for the Legal Process scholars. It would mean asking judges to act as political agents, which is precisely what the Legal Realists claimed they did and what the Legal Process scholars were trying to defend against.

Like utilitarianism, Rousseau's version of the social contract is analytically helpful to the extent that it structures the way we think about political and moral theory. But it is void of specific normative content, so it is not very helpful in deciding particular moral or political issues. Rousseau's technique of making the majority the arbiter of the general will does not give us much help in determining how we should vote on a particular issue. It is not very helpful to a judge trying to apply a background moral theory to resolve ambiguities on the surface of our legal norms.

THERE IS, HOWEVER, a deeper way in which Rousseau's social contract affects our moral analysis of law. In a subtle but important way, Rousseau changes our conception of freedom. Liberty is not freedom from any constraint; it is the ability to engage in self-rule. It is obedience to self-imposed constraints. These self-imposed constraints are the product of decisions free from individual biases and inclinations. They are the product of public reason, free from the influences of individual appetites and passions in the real world.

This idea seems to resonate with everyday moral and political discourse. If we are debating a political issue, we often admonish the participants to divorce themselves from their own particular circumstances. We will see more of this when we discuss Rawls. We will see at a deeper level Rousseau's conception of freedom as following the dictates of reason free from inclination when we discuss Kant.

Suppose I decide through cerebral reflection that I want to be healthier and more fit. One way to do that is to eat healthier food. But then on the way to work, I pass a bakery and its aromas of freshly baked pastries. Should I defer to my immediate desires and appetites and eat the pastry? Or should I "constrain" myself by deferring to reason and my judgment that I should eat healthier foods? It is plausible to conclude that I am freer (more autonomous) if I constrain myself from going into the bakery. Odysseus was more autonomous by tying himself to the mast so that the Sirens would not lure him to his death.[45] Aren't each of us more autonomous by having a life plan for who we want to become and then sticking to the plan? We might debate whether this notion of autonomy is more authentic than any other, but it is certainly plausible. It is even powerful. We shall see it more clearly in Kant. It started with Rousseau.

This conception of freedom allows Rousseau to say that we can force people to be free.[46] Freedom is not merely giving into all of our brute desires and appetites; it is living according to a set of decisions given to us by reason free from those inclinations. We can force people to be free by not allowing them to live simply according to their appetites. Of course, this conception of freedom can also be dangerous. Lenin's doctrine of the dictatorship of the proletariat is an example,[47] exercising gruesome coercion with the idea that it will transform people in a way that the coercion can later be abandoned with the withering away of the state. Nevertheless, we see in Rousseau that some constraints help us shape ourselves and our society in ways that we freely decide they should go. Law, family, and education shape us, so we should take control and shape them. This is a profound idea, and it leads us to Kant.

IMMANUEL KANT WAS born in Königsberg, a university town in East Prussia, and he spent most of his life there. Legend has it that his neighbors could set their watches by his afternoon constitutional. One day he did not appear. It was the day that he received Rousseau's *Emile.*[48] If Kant was motivated in much of his philosophy to respond to the work of David Hume, he seems to have been enamored with Rousseau. Building on Rousseau, Kant built a social contract theory of his own. He relied on Rousseau but also addressed many of Rousseau's shortcomings.

Kant's philosophy is much broader and deeper than Rousseau's. Indeed, he is one of the deepest and most profound philosophers in the Western tradition. Much of his work addresses the problem of epistemology—how we know things. A pervasive view in the Western tradition has been that we know things just to the extent that our ideas about the world correspond to the objective reality of the world. Going back to the pre-Socratic philosophers in Greece, there has been a sharp distinction between the subject—the person trying to understand the world—and the object—the thing that the subject is trying to understand. Kant challenged that view by arguing that humans—as subjects—bring certain concepts to our understanding of the world that enable us to understand it. Our concepts help shape our understanding of the world. This is sometimes called the "Copernican revolution" in philosophy.[49] Just as Copernicus put the sun at the center of the celestial universe, Kant put humans back at the center of philosophy.

Kant also distinguished between the "noumenal" world—the world as it actually is—and the "phenomenal" world—the world as we experience it. We will return to these ideas later. The point here is that Kant's social contract theory was a small part of his enormous overall contribution to philosophical thought.

SO WHAT DID Kant think about law and moral philosophy? He addressed these topics in two important works: *Groundwork of the Metaphysics of Morals,*[50] and *The Metaphysical Elements of Justice.*[51] Basic to Kant's moral philosophy is a notion of freedom that he got from Rousseau's notion of moral freedom. Rousseau's notion applies to citizens of a legitimate state. Their freedom consists in their obeying laws they give to themselves collectively as the supreme legislature of a direct democracy, provided those laws express the general will. Kant extracted this notion from the context of a particular political society and applied it to human beings generally. Kant held that every rational being, by virtue of being rational, is capable of governing himself or herself by laws of his or her own making.[52] To live according to such laws is to be autonomous. Every rational being, then, by virtue of his or her powers of reason, is capable of autonomy. Kant explained this notion of freedom as autonomy of the will.[53] Such autonomy is the source of intrinsic or absolute value, which all of humanity has and which is distinct from the relative value that objects have for human beings depending on their desires. Accordingly, Kant identified the former as dignity and the latter as price.[54] Autonomy of the will is a positive notion of freedom. Such freedom is possible, Kant held, because the will of a rational agent can be determined solely by laws of its own making. Though Kant held that such freedom is possible, he denied that we could ever experience it. In other words, he took this positive notion to be a notion of noumenal freedom. Kant distinguished it from the notion of the will not being subject to determination by natural forces.[55] This negative notion is the traditional notion of freedom of the will. Kant, following tradition, held that we are conscious of having such freedom. In other words, he took this negative notion to be a notion of phenomenal freedom.

His main thesis in explaining how a metaphysical grounding of morality is possible was that these two notions of freedom are reciprocal. Everything in the universe, Kant maintained, works according to laws.[56] Natural forces work according to the laws of causation that determine events in the phenomenal world. They work, that is, according to the laws of nature. Consequently, if something is not subject to determination by natural forces, then its operations are not regulated by the laws of nature. It is regulated instead by a different kind of law. Thus, if the will is free in the sense of its not being determined by natural forces, then laws of a different kind must regulate its operations. These are laws that the will, as the cause of its operations, gives to itself. In other words, the autonomy of the will follows from the will being free in the sense of its not being determined by natural forces. Conversely, if the will is autonomous, then, being the cause of its operations, those operations are regulated by laws that the will gives to itself. They are not regulated by the laws of nature. Its operations, in other words, are not determined by natural forces. Thus, negative freedom of the will follows from the will being autonomous.

Kant used this reciprocal relation between the positive and negative notions of freedom as the springboard for the argument he gave to show that every rational agent, by virtue of being rational, is capable of governing himself or herself by laws of his or her own making. The argument is at the foundation of his moral philosophy. To act rationally, Kant declared, is to act under an idea of freedom.[57] One cannot, that is, understand oneself as acting rationally or identify one's action as the result of a reasoned choice if one thought the reasoning that informed one's choice was the product of purely mechanical forces. Consequently, from a practical point of view, every rational agent is free. The freedom one attributes to oneself qua rational agent, from this point of view, is in the first instance negative since it consists in the understanding of reason as free from determination by mechanical forces. But given the thesis that the two notions of freedom, negative and positive, are reciprocal, one must also attribute to oneself, qua rational agent, positive freedom. And such an attribution means affirming the autonomy of one's will as necessary to one's being a rational agent. Thus, through this understanding of one's will, one conceives of oneself as a moral agent, an agent who acts by laws of his or her own making.

Kant built his moral theory on this idea of the autonomy of the will. The argument is sometimes obscure but seems to proceed something like this. The laws one gives to oneself in the exercise of one's autonomy are universal moral principles. To be universal, these principles must have what has absolute value as their ground. Only the will of an autonomous agent has such value, so the principles require action that treats every human being as having absolute value or, in Kant's words, as an end. This requirement is expressed in one of the formulations Kant gives to the principle of morality that is at the foundation of his system: *Act in such a way that you treat humanity, whether in your own person or in the person of another, always as an end and never merely as a means.*[58] In Kant's theory, the foundational principle of morality is the Categorical Imperative, and this formulation of it is commonly referred to as "the formula of humanity."

The formula of humanity contains two directives: never treat people merely as means, and always treat them as ends. Kant identifies the first with the principle of justice. It establishes the basis of a just political order. The principle requires that one exercise one's will in such a way that one's own freely made choices can coexist, in accordance with universal law, with everyone's freedom.[59] In other words, we need to recognize that there are other autonomous agents in the world, so we should always act so that we are part of a kingdom of ends—that we are only one of many autonomous agents in the world.[60] We ought to exercise our own freedom as autonomous agents, but we ought not trample on the freedom of others.[61] We should act so that our exercise of freedom is compatible with the maximum equal ability of others to exercise their freedom.[62] This principle can be satisfied only in a well-regulated—that is, legally regulated—society.

This rendition of Kant's account of the social contract is substantially in line with that of Rousseau, or even with those of Hobbes and Locke. Individuals in a state of nature would willingly give up their natural liberty to secure more reliable protection for life (Hobbes) or property rights (Locke); or they would willingly exchange their natural liberty for moral freedom (Rousseau and Kant).

Kant then gives a further elaboration of our moral duties. If Rousseau simply gave us the general will—which had no content—Kant says that our moral duties are governed by the Categorical Imperative. To show how the Categorical Imperative guides our common moral reasoning, that is, the ordinary way by which we rationally determine our moral duties, Kant uses a different formulation of it, the formula of universal law. This formulation requires individuals to act so that the maxim of their action—the principle corresponding to their plan of action—can be willed to be a universal law.[63] It says that any action is moral, so long as the actor would be willing to let everyone act on the same principle. This looks a bit like the Golden Rule. It outlaws inconsistency and hypocrisy.

An action might violate the Categorical Imperative in one of two different ways. First, an action, if the maxim on which it was done were followed by everyone, might actually be impossible to do.[64] If I want to lie for my own personal benefit, I would have to imagine a world in which everyone lies for their own personal benefit. But in that world no one would rely on other people's statements. Then it would be impossible to fool anyone by lying, which is precisely what the proposed maxim describes.

In other cases, this sort of logical inconsistency would not occur. Suppose that I want to spit on the sidewalk. I would have to be willing to let everyone spit on the sidewalk. That maxim would not be inconsistent with itself. Even if everyone spit on the sidewalk, I could still do so. But this conduct might violate the Categorical Imperative in another way. The Categorical Imperative would require that, as a normative matter, I would be willing to let everyone else spit on the sidewalk. If I were not, my conduct would violate the Categorical Imperative.[65] This seems to be a standard that outlaws hypocrisy.

MUCH HAS BEEN written about whether Kant makes a good case for the Categorical Imperative.[66] No consensus among scholars has been reached. But assuming that he has, what are its implications for the questions we have been asking? First, the state is clearly permitted morally to impose a legal system on its citizens. A legal regime is necessary to protect maximum equal liberty and therefore to satisfy the principle of justice. Moreover, Kant makes the coercion of our legal system compatible with human freedom. It is, after all, a requirement that flows from the autonomy of the will—that is, from the dictates of pure reason free from determination by inclination.

Second, individuals seem to have an absolute obligation under the Categorical Imperative to obey the law.[67] In order to disobey the law, an individual would have to posit a maxim that she was willing to make a universal law. But that would mean everyone could disobey the law, and the rule of law would break down. Since law is necessary to fulfill the principle of justice, that would be unacceptable. In fact, Kant has a lengthy discussion of these obligations in the *Metaphysical Elements of Justice.*[68] He explicitly states that individuals have an absolute obligation to obey the law. And if there is a revolution or a coup that replaces the government, then individuals have an absolute obligation to obey the new regime as well.

SO FAR, KANT'S version of the social contract improves on Rousseau's. Kant gives a deeper account of the nature of human freedom as the determination of the will by reason independent of inclination. Rousseau simply posits free will, but Kant gives it a metaphysical explanation as noumenal freedom that operates independently of causal forces that have a phenomenal manifestation. The former operates according to its own laws; the latter operates according to the laws of nature. Kant's metaphysics is not parsimonious because it requires the division between things-in-themselves (noumena) and things-as-experienced (phenomena), just as Plato's metaphysics is not parsimonious because it distinguishes between the world of forms and the world of objects that participate in the forms. But it nonetheless offers some underpinning to the attribution of freedom as a fundamental fact about human nature that he shares with Rousseau. Moreover, Kant did not expound it solely to account for human autonomy. It also has a significant part in his groundbreaking contributions to epistemology.

Kant's version of the social contract improves on Rousseau's in a second and more important way. While both take it as an exchange of the natural liberty people have in the state of nature for the moral freedom they have under the rule of law, Kant further explains the rule of law by giving content to the moral law. All that Rousseau said was that the moral law—the law of a legitimate state—is defined by the general will; the general will did not have any content. It relied on an arbitrary claim that the majority in a democratic republic is the oracle of the general will. Kant, by contrast, gives content to the moral law in the form of the Categorical Imperative. The Categorical Imperative allows for a great deal of flexibility, but it imposes *some* constraints on our behavior.

So maybe Kant's moral theory can do the work that the Legal Process scholars ask of moral theory. Maybe it can resolve ambiguities in legal norms. Even at first blush, however, this appears unlikely. Almost any meaningful legal norm will address issues that require a normative judgment more specific than asking whether we would let everyone act in the same way. To determine whether an ordinance that bans vehicles in the park applies to bicycles, we need to know whether the ordinance was motivated by environmental concerns over safety concerns. It is not enough to ask whether we would be willing to let everyone bring their bicycle to the park. If utilitarianism is hopelessly dependent upon the results of indeterminate analyses of empirical consequences, the Categorical Imperative is hopelessly open.

THERE IS A DEEPER problem. Exactly what does it mean to say that I have to act according to a maxim that I would will to be universal law—that is, that I would be willing to let everyone act on? Suppose I want to eat at a certain restaurant tonight. Would that be immoral because I could not will that to be a universal law? If everyone in the world ate at that restaurant tonight, it would be impossible for me to eat at the restaurant tonight. I want to become a lawyer. I want to marry

Kim. I can't do it if everyone does it. Surely Kant did not mean to outlaw any of that conduct.

An answer could be that I have to be more careful formulating the maxim that informs my conduct. I will eat at this particular restaurant tonight as long as it is not too crowded. Now I am willing to let everyone act on that maxim. It would still be possible for me to do so, so my conduct would not violate the Categorical Imperative.

The problem is that this response proves too much. Suppose that I want to rob a bank. If I do not want to live in a world where everyone robs banks, it seems that I would be unwilling to enact my maxim as a universal law. But suppose my maxim is to bring it about that Bill Powers robs a bank. I might be willing to let everyone act according to *that* maxim. Or suppose I don't want to pay my taxes. I might be willing to allow everyone to act according to the maxim that law professors don't have to pay taxes. And so on.

The application of the Categorical Imperative is dependent on how specific we make the maxim. In the case of my eating at a restaurant, articulating a more specified maxim seems unproblematic. It seems necessary to bring the Categorical Imperative into correspondence with our commonsense intuitions. At the same time, a maxim to bring it about that Bill Powers can rob a bank or that law professors don't have to pay their taxes seems to be "cheating." But there is nothing in Kant's theory that tells us one set of maxims is permissible while the other is not. Intuitively, we can distinguish between eating at a restaurant and robbing a bank, but that is because we are making a moral judgment about these different forms of conduct. We have to make a moral judgment as a prerequisite to applying the Categorical Imperative, but making that moral judgment was supposed to be the role of the Categorical Imperative. If we have to make moral judgments to apply a rule that is supposed to give us moral answers, then the theory isn't doing what it is supposed to do.

We shouldn't be too harsh on the Categorical Imperative. Utilitarianism was hopelessly vague because, among other things, it depended on very indeterminate empirical evaluations of consequences. Nevertheless it helped structure the way we approach moral analysis. It didn't give definitive answers, but it set the ground rules for debating them. Similarly, the Categorical Imperative asks a very powerful moral question: Would you be willing to let everyone else act according to the same principle? An answer to that question might be manipulated, but it still has a powerful impact on how we think about moral problems. Even so, Kant's Categorical Imperative does not seem to do the kind of work that the Legal Process scholars were looking for in terms of a background moral theory resolving ambiguities on the surface of legal norms. Rawls's theory, at first blush, seems better equipped to do it.

JOHN RAWLS PUBLISHED *A Theory of Justice* in 1971.[69] He defends a theory based on Rousseau and Kant. It also includes elements from the utilitarian tradition and insights from economics and game theory. Rawls was in the philosophy department at Harvard when Lon Fuller and Henry Hart were developing their jurisprudential theories at Harvard Law School. He shared with them an interest in justifying principles as the products of fair procedures.

Rawls's argument has two prongs. One is to develop principles of justice that correspond to our intuitive individual moral judgments, much as a mathematician chooses a function to best represent a collection of points on a graph. It might be a straight line, or a sine curve, or a parabola. But then we notice that the points on the graph don't quite match the function. So we reconsider our individual moral intuitions in light of the principles that seem to explain them. Or we might change our principles in light of the fact that they don't quite match our moral judgments. He calls this process "reflective equilibrium."[70] We continue it until we arrive at the best match between attractive principles and attractive individual moral judgments.

This methodology should be familiar to lawyers and law students. It is similar to the process that takes place in the courses law students take in their first year of law school. Through a series of hypotheticals, a class uses the Socratic method to ascertain principles that might explain results in individual cases. The principles might themselves cause us to reevaluate individual judgments, and contrary individual judgments might cause us to reevaluate the principles. This is the methodology of casuistry.

Rawls's second prong builds on the social contract theory of Rousseau and Kant. What principles of justice would be adopted by persons in the "original position"?[71] The original position corresponds to the standpoint of the sovereign in Rousseau's legitimate state or to the standpoint of Kant's kingdom of ends. Individuals in the original position freely adopt principles of justice that will govern social arrangements in the actual world. They arrive at these principles by using reason free from certain types of confounding biases. But Rawls does not insulate individuals in the original position from *all* knowledge about the actual world. They are aware that individuals living in the actual world will have needs and desires. They will develop life plans. They know that there will not be enough goods for everyone to have everything they want, but scarcity will not be so great that they will have to fight just to stay alive. They know some basic facts about human biology and psychology. But they don't know what their own particular life plans will be. They don't know their gender, their physical attributes, or the other characteristics that will affect their particular desires.[72] The occupants of the original position deliberate under a "veil of ignorance."[73] They know enough about the world to give the principles of justice content, but they don't know so much as to bias their decisions in inappropriate ways.

RAWLS THEN PROCEEDS with a lengthy and complex argument about the decisions individuals in the original position would make. He uses economic theory, game theory, and other psychological and sociological insights to conclude that individuals in the original position would adopt two principles of justice.[74] Individuals in the original position will be conservative and favor future flexibility. Not knowing what particular life plans they will have, they prefer to keep their options open. One way to do that is to work liberty into the principles of justice. They will also be wary of inequalities because they won't know which side of the line they will fall. They would not tolerate inequalities between men and women because they don't know their gender. Within limits, they will prefer to have more rather than less, reflecting utilitarianism. So they choose liberty, equality, and utility.

More precisely, individuals in the original position adopt the following two principles of justice.[75] First, each person is to have an equal right to the most extensive basic liberty that is compatible with a similar liberty for others. This is the "maximum equal liberty principle." It is very similar to Kant's principle of justice. It is "lexically" prior to the second principle, by which Rawls means that it must be satisfied before the second principle comes into play (alphabetically azz comes before baa.)[76]

If the first principle is met, the second principle provides that social and economic inequalities are permitted only if they are both (a) reasonably expected to be to everyone's advantage and (b) attached to positions open to all. Rawls observes that both conditions on inequalities are open to different interpretations. The interpretation of (b) that he favors is the principle of fair equality of opportunity, which says that eligibility for positions must be free not only of legal barriers but also of unfair advantages and disadvantages due to people's social circumstances.[77] The interpretation of (a) that Rawls favors is the difference principle, which says that inequalities are limited to circumstances in which the inequality actually works to the maximal benefit of the representative person who comes out worst under the inequality.[78] If an equal distribution would give everyone $10, and an unequal distribution would give most people $50 but give the worst off $12, the latter scheme would be chosen. The worst off is better off. If an unequal distribution gave most people $100 but the worst off $9, the scheme would be rejected. Rawls's argument is that someone in the original position would not complain about an inequality if it made everyone better off. They would not know where they would fall on the distribution, but they would at least know they would be better off no matter what.

Again, the two principles of justice are lexically ordered. Social arrangements cannot trade basic liberties guaranteed by the first principle in order to gain economic advantages under the second principle.[79] It would be unjust to curtail free speech, even if it would make everyone better off economically. (Presumably, an *individual* can trade liberty for economic again, such as by entering a contract, but a social rule cannot do so.) Even inequalities that make everyone better off are prohibited if they rely on criteria that are not "open to all" under conditions of fair equality of opportunity.[80] This captures our repugnance to racial and gender discrimination.

Rawls leaves open whether the core idea behind the difference principle applies to the first principle of justice as well. Would an unequal distribution of liberty be permissible if it actually gave more *liberty* to the group made worse off? It is clear that liberty cannot be traded for economic advantage, but it is not as clear why Rawls would favor strict egalitarianism with respect to liberty but not with respect to economic arrangements.

Before we apply these principles to particular situations, it is useful to note that Rawls differs from Rousseau and Kant and the utilitarians in an important respect. Rousseau and Kant valorize liberty. Equality comes into Rousseau's thinking only at the point where the majority is the oracle of the general will. Everyone has an equal vote. For Kant, equality comes in only with the principle of justice. That our free choices must coexist with everyone's freedom under universal law implies that everyone in a just legal order has an equal claim to liberty. It is not quite clear why that is so, but it does represent a gesture toward equality. But the dominant motivating value for Rousseau and Kant is moral freedom. For the utilitarians, the only intrinsic value is human happiness; equality and liberty do not have any independent moral claim. They are important only if they contingently contribute to happiness.

For Rawls, the two principles of justice essentially reflect our commitment to liberty, to equality, and to happiness (material goods). This is important for reflective equilibrium, because in everyday discourse we hear claims of liberty, equality, and happiness. By including each of them in the principles of justice, Rawls is able to claim that the principles do a reasonably good job of reflecting late-twentieth-century Western moral values. Rawls lives in a pluralistic world. He does provide an algorithm for ordering these competing values, so he does not leave us adrift to explain how they fit together. But he at least recognizes pluralistic values. Metaphorically, he is a polytheist, not a monotheist. We will return to this point in due course.

RAWLS'S TWO PRINCIPLES of justice apply to social arrangements. What about the moral obligations of individuals? Rawls distinguishes between moral "duties" and "obligations." An obligation is undertaken according to the requirements of a particular office or arrangement that an individual voluntarily enters into.[81] An individual who voluntarily becomes a judge and accepts the benefits of the office takes on the obligations it defines. When we have not voluntarily entered into an office or arrangement, we do not have any obligations, but we do have moral duties. We have a moral duty not to injure others, and we also have a moral duty to support reasonably just social institutions, as judged by the two principles of justice.[82]

Rawls seems to make progress in accounting for our moral intuitions. Most of us think that we do take on special obligations when we voluntarily enter into an office or arrangement. We may have moral duties aside from that, but voluntarily undertaking an office adds to the moral calculus. I have certain moral duties toward my neighbors, but I have special moral obligations to students whom I voluntarily undertake to teach.

SO DOES THE STATE have a moral right to coerce its citizens? The two principles of justice suggest that it does. As long as the state enacts laws that reasonably comply with the two principles of justice, it complies with the dictates of morality. Moreover, law itself protects our liberties as demanded by the first principle of justice.

Individuals in the original position choose principles of justice for the regulation of the major political, economic, and social institutions of their society. The principles are thus the basis of a just legal order. Accordingly, laws that deprive people of fundamental rights and liberties are unjust. It would be unjust to pass laws that enacted racial or gender discrimination, because they would attach inequalities to offices not open to all. And it would be unjust to distribute governmental benefits unequally if by doing so the worst off were not made better off. So the state's ability to coerce citizens would depend heavily on the content of its legal regime. But as long as it was reasonably just under the two principles of justice, the state would be justified in imposing a legal regime.

WHAT ARE THE MORAL obligations of an individual with respect to obeying the law? As long as the legal regime is reasonably just under the two principles of justice, an individual has a moral duty to support it. And for some people, like judges, police officers, and lawyers, there is also a specific obligation to obey the rules of the legal system.

An individual might take a granulated approach by claiming that a *particular* law is unjust under the two principles of justice. The individual might claim that there is no moral duty to follow a particular law that violates the two principles of justice and that this violation could take place in a way that still supported the overall legal regime. Civil disobedience, which we discussed in the context of utilitarianism, might be such a method.

THIS BRINGS US to the question with which we began our discussion of moral theories: Do Rawls's two principles of justice do the work desired by the Legal Process scholars of answering the Legal Realists by resolving ambiguities on the surface of legal norms? Rawls's two principles of justice seem, on their face, to have more content than Rousseau's general will or Kant's Categorical Imperative. And they do not appear to raise as many of the empirical questions that affect utilitarianism. (They do raise some, such as whether an inequality actually works to the benefit of the least well-off. But these questions are not as pervasive as in utilitarianism.)

Moreover, Rawls's veil of ignorance offers an improvement on Kant's Categorical Imperative. The Categorical Imperative requires only that an individual act on a maxim that he could will to be a universal law. If one makes the maxim specific enough, one can justify almost any action. The veil of ignorance puts a limit on this. If we require an actor to state the maxim while not knowing where she will fall on any category the maxim creates, she will be cautious about constructing unduly granulated maxims. Would I really be willing to let everyone act on the maxim that men or lawyers get special treatment if I don't know that I will end up being a man or a lawyer?

As it turns out, however, Rawls's two principles of justice do not fare much better at giving determinate answers that might fill the gaps of ambiguous legal norms. Consider the second principle of justice. It calls first for equality in the distribution of goods and services, except only when an inequality meets the difference principle. But what counts as equality? As Peter Westen famously noted in *The Empty Idea of Equality,*[83] equality alone does not provide a definitive answer to the very questions it was designed to address.

Consider a salary structure where executives are paid a multiple of what workers are paid. If this is an inequality, then it is permissible only if it actually makes the workers better off than they would be under a system of equal pay. Maybe astute management will create more profits that can be passed on to workers. But maybe not. But what does equal pay mean? Does it mean equal per person? Equal per hour worked? Equal per effort? Equal per unit of output? Or an equal right to participate in a market process of voluntary bargaining? We can't tell whether a scheme deviates from equality without first agreeing on a substantive standard against which equality is measured. But that requires an answer to the very moral question we thought the second principle of justice was going to answer. So to apply the second principle of justice, we must first decide the moral question we began with. The second principle of justice is not merely ambiguous; it begs the very question it was designed to answer.

And why is the proposed pay structure governed by the second principle of justice at all? Why isn't it governed by the first principle? Why isn't this a question of liberty, not a question of the distribution of goods? The higher-paid workers simply negotiated a higher salary through a voluntary system of market contracts. Objectors would argue that the market is skewed, but that is the very question of social morality that we would expect a theory of justice to answer. It is a problem if we have to answer it before applying the principles of justice themselves.

Maybe the veil of ignorance can help. What if we ask the question about the pay structure from behind the veil of ignorance in the original position? We might argue that individuals in the original position would choose per-capita equality. Equal pay per unit of output or unit of effort would reward people with attributes that produce those results. Just as individuals behind the veil of ignorance would not know their gender, so too would they not know whether they would be talented or hardworking. On the strategy for making decisions in circumstances of uncertainty that Rawls favors, they would want to protect themselves from the worst outcomes. This is known as the "maximin strategy": when deciding in circumstances of uncertainty about the outcomes of taking different options, choose the option whose worst outcome, as compared to the worst outcomes of the other options, is least bad.[84] The choice of per-capita equality would follow on this strategy because they would worry that they might be unskilled or lazy.

But this won't work. For one thing, this result does not comport with our normal moral intuitions under reflective equilibrium. To be sure, there are advocates of a totally equal distribution of goods, irrespective of work, but most people would at least reward effort and hard work. But from the original position, a propensity for hard work is just like any other characteristic about which we are ignorant.

Moreover, there are too many other situations where this approach would lead to results that Rawls would not endorse. What about a system of law that punishes criminals? Why isn't that an unequal distribution of goods that is prohibited by the second principle of justice? The intuitive answer is that this scheme does not constitute an inequality; everyone is being treated equally according to the rule that prohibits criminal behavior. But why is a propensity toward criminal behavior not just one of the characteristics about which we would be ignorant in the original position? True, a system of criminal laws makes the average person better off by establishing order and securing our liberties, but it is unlikely that it makes the criminal better off. So people in the original position, if they follow the maximin strategy, would guard against the possibility that they would end up being a criminal.

The veil of ignorance was intended to be used in the original position to *adopt* the principles of justice. It was not intended to be used in the real world to help *apply* the principles of justice. In any event, with or without the veil of ignorance, we have to find some way to distinguish between rules that discriminate on the basis of criminality and those that discriminate on, say, the basis of gender. It seems obvious that distinctions based on gender are more pernicious than distinctions based on criminality, but the principles of justice themselves don't tell us this. We have to use a preexisting moral judgment about the difference between criminality and gender before we can even apply the two principles of justice.

Rawls's two principles of justice seem as ill-suited to perform the task assigned to a moral theory in the Legal Process School as utilitarianism, Rousseau's general will, and Kant's Categorical Imperative. It is simply not the case, as we go deeper into our moral commitments, that we can resolve ambiguities that we find in the surface of legal norms.

WE NEED NOT overstate these points. It is true that, as we go deeper into our moral commitments, we find that these moral theories have radical ambiguities. They beg the deepest moral questions about our social arrangements that we would expect them to answer. But this does not mean that the Legal Process School has not made significant progress in understanding how legal analysis works. It is still the case that, when we confront an ordinance that, say, prohibits vehicles in the park, we can look to the immediate purpose of the ordinance to help resolve some ambiguities. It is hard to think of any purpose that would exclude a baby buggy. Whether bicycles are precluded depends on whether the statute was motivated by environmental concerns or safety concerns. That might not be clear from the context. But it might be.

This type of purposive analysis is likely to be applicable in a great variety of cases. So the Legal Process School does provide a tool to resolve what seem to be ambiguities on the surface of legal norms in a wide array of cases. Put another way, our legal system is not quite as ambiguous as the Legal Realists claim. In many cases, if not all, there is a hermeneutical methodology that is neither Keen's literalism nor Handy's pure instrumentalism. In many cases, that is, and perhaps all, judges have a middle ground where they are not mere ciphers, but neither are they mere policy makers. They exercise judgment, but they can still claim to be passive to the values of the "author" of the legal norm.

What the Legal Process School is unable to produce is a methodology in which judges can *always* avoid legislating simply by referring to the legal system's background moral purposes. Even here, however, these background moral theories are still helpful. They do not always give definitive answers, but they still do a powerful job framing the debate. Rawls's two principles may not tell us whether gender and criminality are morally different criteria, *but once we make that judgment* the concept of equality is very powerful. Kant's Categorical Imperative might not be definitive, but our asking "What if everyone did that?" is still instructive. Utilitarianism still points to concerns about aggregate welfare.

Still, there does not seem to be a "point" atop any great pyramid of purposes.

EIGHT

HISTORICAL SCHOOLS OF THOUGHT: CRITICAL LEGAL STUDIES AND POSTMODERN LEGAL THEORIES

LEGAL REALISTS OBSERVED that legal norms are often ambiguous on the surface. Judges resolve these ambiguities by inserting their own policy or political preferences, thereby opening themselves to the accusation that they are acting like legislators. Adherents to the Legal Process School then answered by referring to purpose, and even shared background moral commitments, to resolve these ambiguities. The ambiguity of the word 'vehicle' in the ordinance banning vehicles from the park can be resolved by looking to the ordinance's purposes—reducing pollution or creating a safe environment for children. But when we delved deeper into moral theories like utilitarianism and various versions of social contract theory, we discovered that the moral theories themselves had irresolvable ambiguities.

This type of critique continues throughout the late twentieth century. It takes a deeper turn with postmodernism and Critical Legal Studies. These movements challenge more than particular moral or political theories. They challenge any enterprise of interpreting texts or data. The basic idea of postmodern theories is that interpreting any text depends on a preexisting ideology the reader brings to the task. This is true for literary texts, cultural values, moral theories, historical data, and, most important for our discussion, legal material such as statutes and cases.

The Critical Legal Studies movement had a decidedly political bent. It grew out of political movements in the 1960s.

Almost everyone in the Critical Legal Studies movement was politically on the left. This caused many people on the right and in the center to dismiss Critical Legal Studies without actually giving its jurisprudential points much serious thought. Critiques of the movement's scholarship often make a caricature of it. Sometimes it seemed that they were claiming that Critical Legal Studies held that law, or other texts, had no meaning at all or that everything, including the physical world, is socially constructed. Much of the legal academy had a cartoonish view of postmodernism and Critical Legal Studies that was easy to ridicule and dismiss. This was a mistake. The leading figures in the Critical Legal Studies movement, like Duncan Kennedy and Jack Balkin, were extremely insightful in their understanding of law and legal interpretation. One did not have to accept their political conclusions to appreciate their jurisprudential insights. Moreover, the work of other postmodern philosophers and political theorists—like Jacques Derrida and Michel Foucault—was extremely deep, whatever its political content.

Early work in Critical Legal Studies was little more than an application of ideas that we have already examined. Recall that applying the concept of equality to a particular problem depended entirely on a prior moral or political commitment of the person doing the evaluating. To someone who believes in a free market, equality might mean an equal opportunity to compete in a laissez-faire market. To someone who believes in the value of hard work, it might mean equal pay per hour worked. To someone who believes in egalitarianism, it might mean equal pay per person, regardless of how much they worked or provided. The concept of equality does not resolve the issue. A person's preexisting political commitments do.

People with different underlying value systems will bring different underlying political commitments to any task of interpretation, including the task of interpreting legal materials. An individual's political views will correlate with their experiences and background. Consequently, different groups of people will come to different conclusions when interpreting the same material. Women will have different views about gender equality than men; people of color will have different views of racial and ethnic equality than whites; and homosexuals will have different views of sexual equality than heterosexuals. Critical Legal Studies scholars analyzed different areas of law from these different perspectives. It is not just that people in different groups will argue for different substantive results, though that is undoubtedly true. It is that they will actually interpret the same materials differently because of the different ideologies each interpreter brings to the task. Thus, we get scholarship in critical race theory, critical gender theory, queer theory, and so on.

This approach to legal interpretation is little different from what we saw in chapter 5. It combines the interpretational ambiguities we saw before with particular political views about feminism, racial justice, and gay rights. The tone of much of the scholarship was that it was especially avant-garde, and its strong political bent caused a negative reaction among conservative elements of the legal profession. But it was not particularly avant-garde jurisprudentially. It claimed that the legal norms and structures of bourgeois liberal society in the late twentieth century were not "naturally" necessary, and judges applying them were not merely "neutral" arbiters of legal disputes. We have seen all of this before.

BUT WITHIN SOME Critical Legal Studies scholarship there was also a profoundly new and avant-garde strand of jurisprudence. Indeed, it was not just jurisprudence in the normal sense. It was a theory of how language and interpretation work generally, not just in law. Law is one field of interpretation among many that formed a general discipline of hermeneutics.[1] The leading proponents were Duncan Kennedy, primarily in his seminal article "Form and Substance in Private Law Adjudication,"[2] and Jack Balkin, primarily in his Yale law review article on Jacques Derrida.[3]

Any statement about the world is a statement within our language system. Its meaning always depends on unstated aspects of that language. If we talk about human freedom, we might not say anything about slavery or determinism, but they are always in the background. We cannot understand the concept of freedom without implicitly understanding those concepts as well. As Derrida put it, the absence is the presence. Determinism and slavery are present even when they are not explicitly invoked. So statements about the world, particularly the moral world, can be "deconstructed" to show that they always mean more (and less) than appears on the surface.

Balkan uses an example of contractual theory, specifically the contract theory of Patrick Atiya.[4] He interprets a long line of contracts cases to conclude that subjective consent forms the paradigm for a contract. Contracts without subjective consent, based on reasonable reliance, are "exceptions" to the normal rule. But we could just as easily see reasonable reliance as forming the normal rule, relegating cases that depend on subjective consent as the exception. Derrida would call this "privileging" one of the concepts over the other. Privileging subjective consent over reliance as an interpretation of contracts law is a normative choice, albeit often an unconscious one. It is not simply a "neutral" or "objective" reading of the material.

Every active interpretation has this feature. It is much like a picture of two red faces looking at each other on a blue background, which could instead be seen as a blue urn on a red background. What counts is that there is no objectively true foreground or background in this picture. One is just privileged over the other. Thus, there is always a subjective and normative element to any interpretation; it is never purely objective and factual.

Even this aspect of Critical Legal Studies—or of Derrida—was not entirely new. It drew (sometimes implicitly) on the tradition of American Pragmatism espoused by William James, John Dewey, and Josiah Royce. It even has roots in Ralph Waldo Emerson and Walt Whitman. In the late twentieth century, its principal proponent was Richard Rorty. Like Balkin and Derrida, the American Pragmatists claimed that the truth of a statement did not consist in its correspondence to the world. It consisted rather in how the statement functioned in conjunction with other statements that collectively represented a useful web of beliefs. Language works systematically; it does not merely break down into individual statements that mirror the "objective" world.

This is the claim that helps form the caricature of Critical Legal Studies: statements can be made to mean anything we want. The table is not really there. But the claim is not that language does not have *any* connection to "reality." If it didn't, it would not be very "useful." The scientific language of quantum mechanics would not make useful predictions if it did not correspond to the world in some useful way. People who wish the "real" chair away will end up with lots of bruises. The Pragmatists and Critical Legal Studies scholars think only that language is not *merely* a set of signs that are concatenated to produce a neutral, objective mirror of "reality."

WE MIGHT ASPIRE to have a legal system with certain features. We might want law to be objectively determined. We might want it to be entirely external to the decision maker. We might want it to be entirely neutral across all of the values about which we might differ. We might want it to be immutable. We might want it to be entirely autonomous from other disciplines. We might want it to exist in nature and not just be a human artifact. This strand of Critical Legal Studies says law does not have any of these features. And this is not true only of law. It is also true of literary theory, philosophy, political rhetoric, and even supposedly factual statements about the world. But this view is not new. Critical Legal Studies scholars were not alone in expounding it. So too did the Pragmatists.

Balkin makes clear that the cartoonish view of Critical Legal Studies as nihilistic is misguided. The fact that our linguistic discourse privileges one interpretation over another does not mean that, within our conventional way of thinking, we don't have meaning or truth. All Balkin and Derrida claim is that meaning and truth are to some extent a matter of (collective) choice. They are not objectively given by a relation of correspondence to the world.

CRITICAL LEGAL STUDIES is a "postmodern" approach. Why do we say that? This takes us back to the beginnings of Western philosophy and to Plato and the earlier pre-Socratics. Balkin makes this very point. Derrida has bigger fish to fry than mere legal theory. He aims to challenge the Platonic idea of objectivity.

Thales of Miletus lived in the sixth century BCE. Before that, most Greeks understood the world through stories and myths. Thales wanted to have an explanation that depended on observation and reason. He was proto-scientific. So he asked, "What is the world made of?" His answer was water. This seems to be naïve, but it is actually quite clever. Ordinary people encounter solids, liquids, and gases. What is the one thing that we observe in ordinary life in all three phases? Water. But the importance of Thales is not his answer. It is his methodology. Moreover, it is the fact that he wanted to find an "objective" answer, one that is the same no matter who made the observation or told the story. By searching for objectivity, Thales was looking for a way of understanding the world that transcended individual observers.

Thales started a tradition that led up to Socrates and Plato. We have only snippets about people between Thales and Plato, so it is not easy to ascertain exactly what they thought. Mostly we have notes taken by their students. They themselves did not write. Only face-to-face conversation was true intellectual engagement. Simply reading someone's book was too passive and detached. Although Plato wrote his ideas down, he did so in the form of dialogues. We might not be talking to Plato, but at least we are reading about people who are in an intellectual conversation. Moreover, most of the snippets we have are *class* notes. Even today teachers often say provocative things in class that are designed to get students to think, even if the teacher does not believe them. So it is difficult to attribute precision to pre-Socratic thinkers. What is clearer, however, is what Plato thought their ideas were.

Parmenides's basic tenet was that reality is unitary and logical. He could not explain change logically, so it did not actually exist. Thus, we have Zeno's paradox. Achilles's arrow would never reach its target because it would go halfway, then another halfway, and then another halfway an infinite number of times. Since it had to traverse an infinite number of segments, it would never arrive. If we seem to observe arrows reaching their target, it must be an illusion. Change does not *really* occur.

Heraclitus was at the other extreme. His famous aphorism was that you can never step in the same stream twice. After all, it would have different bits of water, a different level of the water, different eddies, and so on. For Heraclitus, everything was change and flux.

Another group of ancient Greek thinkers taught rhetoric and persuasive argumentation to the sons of wealthy families in Athens so they could be successful orators in the legal and policy debates that took place in the Athenian assembly. These were the Sophists, such as Gorgias and Protagoras, each of whom finds his way into a Platonic dialogue. Their sin was teaching for money rather than teaching as a search for truth—as a *philosopher* would do. They taught either side of an argument so that it would be persuasive. The rap on the Sophists was much like the rap on lawyers today. The persuasiveness of language was all that counted.

Protagoras said that "man is the measure of all things."[5] In one sense, this is undeniable. Whether a surface is hot depends on whether we are accustomed to colder surfaces or hotter surfaces. Maybe this is all Protagoras meant. But maybe he meant that man is the measure of *all* things, even in ethics. This type of moral relativism would have been very disturbing to Socrates and Plato, because they wanted to establish enduring, objective, moral principles.

IN ANY EVENT, this was the intellectual context for Socrates and his disciple Plato. People who read or hear about Plato think that he is enormously abstract and otherworldly. Indeed, Raphael's famous painting *The Academy at Athens* in the Vatican shows Plato pointing toward the heavens and the more down-to-earth Aristotle pointing toward the ground. But Plato had a pragmatic, real-world problem that he had inherited from Parmenides and Heraclitus. Common sense (based on our experience) tells us that things change, but they also have continuity over time. My friend has changed over the last several years, but he is still the same person. The Mississippi River changed even over the last week, but it is still the Mississippi River. How can we explain both change and continuity? That problem is not so otherworldly after all.

Plato's solution is his famous theory of the forms. The forms exist in an ideal realm. Objects in "our" world, such as horses, streams, and triangles, are imperfect and changing "shadows" of these forms, just like the objects on the wall in the allegory of the cave are shadows of a deeper reality lurking behind the inhabitants. Objects in our world do change, but the forms they are shadows of do not. Consequently, Heraclitus's stream is changing in our world, but its form has continuity. Whether or not this is an attractive solution to the problem of change and continuity—even Plato came to have serious doubts in the *Parmenides*—it is at least an attempt to make sense of a practical real-world problem.

Plato thought that both this world and the realm of the forms are real. Objects in our world are discovered through observation. The forms are discovered through reason and Socratic dialogue. In *The Republic,* Plato shows us how to get closer to the form of justice through Socratic dialogue—that is, through reasoned speech or *logos.* We have a method to access an objective world that transcends each of us as an individual subject. The Sophists took a different approach. For them, language was everything. They were not interested in ascertaining an objective truth that transcends individual subjects.

This distinction was the foundation of Western philosophy for two and a half millennia. Plato espoused a philosophy of *being.* There are actual things that exist independent of our minds that our minds have (possibly feeble) access to. This is why Alfred North Whitehead said that everything in Western philosophy is just a footnote to Plato. This is the foundation that Balkin says that Derrida is trying to overturn.

THIS BASIC STRUCTURE of Western philosophy takes a number of twists and turns through the millennia. An important one, of course, was the turn to epistemology, the theory of how we know things. In the seventeenth century, René Descartes tried to put our knowledge of the external world on firm footing: I think, therefore I am. But this took a pivotal turn in the late eighteenth century with Kant's "Copernican revolution." For Plato, there was a rigorous separation between subject and object. The object existed unchanged regardless of the activities or perceptions of the subject. For Kant, however, the subject came to the center of how we understand the world. The real or unvarnished world—the noumenal world—cannot be comprehended directly. We form and understand the phenomenal world through our concepts of space, time, and causation. These are concepts *we* bring to our understanding of the world. We are the ones who shape the noumenal world into the phenomenal that obeys the laws of causation and physics.

We can now see how this Kantian pivot leads to the ambiguities we saw in chapter 7. When we try to apply concepts like equality, it is not merely the concept of equality doing the work. We put our preexisting ideas about the market, hard work, and egalitarianism to work as well. What one person thinks is equality will differ from what another person thinks. This lacks the objectivity that Plato was striving for. This wasn't a problem for Kant, because he thought the concepts we bring to the table are the same for every rational being. But Kant still opened the door by putting the subject at the center of how we understand the world.

A SUBJECT-CENTERED approach has permeated almost every field of hermeneutics where we are trying to ascertain meaning. In his later philosophy as a theory of language, Wittgenstein says that meaning depends not on the logical definitions of words but rather on the context and purpose or their customary use. In his famous example of asking the sitter to teach one's children a game, it is only the context—including the social practices of culture in which the statement is made—that makes us realize that the word "game" here does not include sex games or war games. This does not mean that any interpretation is as good as the next. In fact, we all understand clearly that the word 'game' here does not include sex games and war games. Wittgenstein's point is that it is not a logical definition that makes this meaning clear; it is our social practices.

So it is in literary theory. Consider, for example, William Blake's poem "London":

I wander thro' each charter'd street,
Near where the charter'd Thames does flow,
And mark in every face I meet
Marks of weakness, marks of woe.

In every cry of every Man,
In every Infants cry of fear,
In every voice, in every ban,
The mind-forg'd manacles I hear

How the Chimney-sweepers cry
Every blackning Church appalls
And the hapless Soldiers sigh,
Runs in blood down Palace walls

But most thro' midnight streets I hear
How the youthful Harlots curse
Blasts the new-born Infants tear
And blights with plagues the Marriage hearse[6]

Blake condemns three human-created institutions. Governments cause wars, churches tolerate and even cause poverty, and marriage marginalizes outsiders. Is Blake's condemnation limited to these three social institutions? Or are these just three examples of a larger critique of society? There is nothing in the poem itself that dictates a narrow or broad reading. Jesus works with the lepers. Is this just a commentary on the plight of leprosy? Or is it a broader message to help the less fortunate and downtrodden?

Sometimes texts themselves give us clues about how to read them, such as when the Book of Deuteronomy overlays a particular philosophy onto Israelite history: our covenant with God is conditional, so those who sin get punished. Or Jesus speaks in parables, which suggests a figurative rather than literal reading. But very often texts are open about how we interpret them. Thus, the reader becomes an important ingredient in forming the meaning of a literary text.

Where should we look to resolve ambiguity in Blake's meaning? Should we look only at the text? Should we look at the historical context? Should we look at Blake's notes or an account of a conversation he had with a friend later in his life? Or should we look to the conventions of our culture? In fact, it seems obvious that "London" has the broader meaning. That is because our culture expects poetry to use metaphors to raise broader issues. Our *culture* has a convention of interpretation. We have been taught in our society how to read poetry. People don't write poetry to make narrow points. They use examples of metaphors to make larger points. So, to be sure, part of the interpretation is in the mind of the beholder, but we share a convention of interpretation that leads to agreement. That is what jurisprudence is about. Does our legal culture have conventions of interpretation?

In literary criticism we find different schools of thought, analogous to jurisprudential schools of thought. They include Formalism, Structuralism, Historicism, and New Criticism (Social Context). We see similar issues crop up in almost every discipline. In science, Thomas Kuhn tells us, scientific theory is formed in paradigms, where the different aspects of knowledge they represent fit together in a particularly coherent way.[7] We understand electrons, or quarks, or strings not on their own but because they fit into a particularly coherent or beautiful theory. We have Werner Heisenberg's famous uncertainty principle (where we cannot measure exactly both the momentum and position of a particle at the same time) and Kurt Gödel's incompleteness theorem in mathematics (that any axiom system for arithmetic that is consistent cannot be complete). In history, what is the meaning of the past? During the Korean War, there was an adage that if Julius Caesar were commanding the troops, he would have nuked the Chinese, that is, he would have been more aggressive. One response might have been that, actually, he would have used catapults. How much can we extrapolate from particulars to make more generalized conclusions? In each area, meaning seems less than absolutely determinate.

ALMOST TWENTY YEARS ago we had a weeklong conference at the University of Texas, "Law and the Other Performing Arts." Sandy Levinson from the law school and Bob Freeman, who was dean of the College of Fine Arts, were the sources of its inspiration. The idea was that problems of interpretation cut across many fields. Judges interpret statutes and cases. Conductors interpret musical compositions written by composers. Directors interpret the works of playwrights, which in turn are interpreted by actors. They use similar techniques. They look at the words (or notes). They look at the overall structure of a text. They look at the social and historical contexts. They might even look at a diary or other hints left behind by the authors. They don't just interpret; they perform. They *decide* cases, or *perform* a symphony, or *perform* a play. They often "translate" earlier material in a way that makes sense for a slightly different setting.

An interpreter or performer brings his or her values to the enterprise. An interpreter or performer is not a purely passive entity reading an objective truth about what the text "really" means. The performer or interpreter adds to the process. There is never a purely neutral interpretation of a Beethoven symphony that captures the "original" meaning. It was avant-garde originally. It is nostalgic today. A dramatic example is "The Grand Inquisitor" in *The Brothers Karamazov*.[8] When

Christ returns and the priest confronts him, the priest tells him that his opinion no longer counts. Christ had his day. Now it is up to the Church to make the interpretation. Fyodor Dostoyevsky may have been critiquing this, but it highlights the role of the interpreter as giving meaning to a text.

There have been many attempts to shore up purely objective meaning. Anthropologists like Claude Lévi-Strauss argued that, while there is relativism from one culture to the next, at the deepest structural level there are similarities.[9] Maybe these structural similarities, at least, represented an objective truth about deep cultural structures. But the act of identifying these structural similarities was itself an active interpretation, subject to all of the subjective issues we have seen before. Thus, we sometimes say we are in a "poststructuralist" as well as a "postmodern" era. The "modern" project, building on Plato and Descartes, was to put our knowledge of an objective world on a sound epistemological footing. Those days seem to be over.

LIKE ALL OF THE THEORIES we have studied, this too has problems. It claims that truth and meaning occur not in an absolute objective sense but as a "useful" part of a system of linguistic (including the words) and cultural conversations. But isn't Plato part of our linguistic and cultural conversations? Maybe a philosophical commitment to language mirroring "reality" is itself a useful way to look at the world. Maybe it gives a more satisfying or otherwise useful outlook on the human condition. Maybe it spawns better behavior. If a Pragmatist responds that a Platonic outlook is just wrong, she would seem to be making the same error she is criticizing. But the point here is not to resolve all of these debates; it is to familiarize ourselves with the positions in them.

Lawyers see postmodernism in their day-to-day work. Consider the problem of interpreting a contract or of trying to ascertain truth from testimony in a courtroom. We have a whole variety of very pragmatic rules about how to go about these processes. We have complicated rules about hearsay evidence.

We have other pragmatic rules of evidence, such as the "best evidence" rule, that are designed to take into account the administrative needs of the courtroom and psychological realities about how juries behave. In contract interpretation, we have the statute of frauds and the "plain meaning" rule, including complicated rules about how extrinsic evidence can be used to resolve an ambiguity but not to create one.

These rules are not based on a belief that they intrinsically represent truth. They are justified by practical benefits of helping people rely on contracts and by establishing efficient ways of resolving disputes. We want to get at something *like* the truth, but these rules of interpretation also reflect the values of reliance and efficiency. In other words, interpretation is in part a pragmatic way to make decisions so we can move forward. This is a far cry from the Platonic project. Indeed, it tends to reflect the pragmatism and problem-solving posture of the Sophists.

SO WHAT ABOUT THE IDEA that we are ruled by laws and not by men? It seems to be in trouble. But the relativism and indeterminacy of these postmodern and poststructuralist theories have been grossly overrated in a cartoonish fashion, just as the philosophical implications of Heisenberg's uncertainty principle and Gödel's incompleteness theorem have been grossly misinterpreted. Heisenberg doesn't say that we cannot know things about the world. He simply says that there are two *particular* things about the world—a subatomic particle's position and momentum—that are entangled in a way that affects our knowledge of *them*. Even with Gödel, we can prove mathematical theorems with absolute certainty. Two plus two is still four. And similarly with law, there are many legal principles that we can all agree on as being true in the legal sense. The president has to be at least thirty-five years old. For the purpose of banning vehicles from the park, a baby buggy is not a vehicle. And so on. These may be true due to conventions of interpretation, but they are still (legally) true.

Interpretation is an active performance, but it is not entirely solipsistic. We share many interpretive values because we live in the same culture. Indeed, one of the functions of law school is to train and inculcate lawyers with shared modes of interpretation. Whether the rule of law will "work" or not depends on how good a job we do. Rousseau saw that in *Emile.* If we want to have a certain kind of society, we had better pay attention to how we educate the next generation.

NINE

METHODOLOGICAL POLYTHEISM

WE HAVE SEEN that there is indeterminacy and subjectivity in any type of interpretation, including in legal interpretation. But there sometimes is a tacit assumption that at least one "mode" of interpretation is the right one, even if it has its own ambiguities. We might disagree about what that mode is, but we seem to assume there is a right answer to that question. Each justice in "The Case of the Speluncean Explorers" thought the other justices were wrong, not only about the result but also about the method they used to arrive at that result. Justice Tatting was paralyzed because he could not decide which method was the proper one to use. Different modes of interpretation can lead to different results. That is yet another source of ambiguity.

We yearn for an integrated and cohesive understanding of the world. In physics, we long for a coherent theory that will integrate gravity with quantum mechanics and the (so far) other three forces: the electromagnetic force, the strong force, and the weak force. Nobel Prizes have been awarded for integrating only two of them. Isaac Newton didn't discover gravity; he discovered that the same force that makes apples fall kept the moon in orbit. James Maxwell integrated electricity and magnetism and then realized that light was just an electromagnetic wave. Emmy Noether discovered that symmetries in physics were the same thing as laws of conservation. We could go on and on. Intellectual progress is largely the quest for ever more general explanations. That was the Platonic project. The theory of the forms explained continuity and change! Aquinas tried to integrate reason and faith!

We see this urge in normative discourse. We might call it the "capstone gambit." We make a series of moral judgments, but we want to say they all fit together under one moral theory, such as utilitarianism. We do this even though that "capstone" standard is hopelessly vague or has other problems. At least we can sleep at night thinking that there is one standard, albeit one that doesn't give us specific answers. There may be a plurality of magical rings in Middle Earth, but there is one ring to rule them all.[1]

We see this most spectacularly in monotheism. In early Israelite theology, Yahweh is probably one of many gods. He has an entourage in heaven and probably has a consort. But after Isaiah, Israelite theology is monotheistic. In the Christian era, it is necessary to understand the Trinity as being compatible with monotheism. We want one god, with one standard. It gives us a unified understanding of the world.

When we try to understand our daily lives, we use different narratives. Consider a hurricane like Katrina. What happened? One way to understand it is that the earth tilts on its axis, causing more sunlight in the summer. The oceans heat up, and so on. Science. Or we can ask why the levees were placed where they were. Human agency. Or ask why God would let this happen. Theology. But if science rules the world, what happens to God or free will? If God is omniscient and omnipotent, what happens to free will and science?

A great deal of philosophy and literature tries to sort out these tensions. Augustine says God gave us free will. In *Oedipus Rex*, Sophocles shows us a world where the Fates control, but Oedipus has choices. We could go on and on. We want to reconcile these seemingly conflicting narratives, even though we live our daily lives perfectly well "believing" in science, free will, and (for some people) God. We can't intellectually reconcile them, but we assume, with Saint Paul, that although we see now through a glass darkly, someday we will see clearly. We crave a unitary, coherent explanation.

But when we think we have one, it erodes. Plato gave up on the theory of the forms in *The Parmenides* and his later dialogues. Aquinas didn't finish *Summa Theologica.* Critical Legal Studies exposes problems in the Legal Process School. London Bridge is falling down. Build it up, but it will fall down again.

Hubert Dreyfus and Sean Kelly tackle this issue in *All Things Shining.*[2] Before Plato, and before Judeo-Christian-Islamic monotheism, the Greeks had the world of Homer. It was decidedly polytheistic. It cherished many things, not just "beauty" but many different beautiful things. This ended with Plato and monotheism. For Dreyfuss and Kelly, Captain Ahab in *Moby Dick* destroys himself searching for the one Good. Ishmael appreciates the many good things (the many shiny things) that surround him without trying to understand them as a unitary system. As Gerard Manley Hopkins put it, "Glory be to dappled things."[3] Or for the French: liberty, fraternity, equality! Rawls got us part way there with freedom, equality, and welfare, but he still thought he needed an algorithm to adjudicate them.

A critical word of caution: philosopher and legal scholar Brian Leiter once reminded me that the point of science—indeed, all intellectual inquiry—is to *try* to find connections, to find general principles that explain theretofore disparate phenomena. Maxwell's integration of electricity and magnetism was a great leap forward. System builders are crucial. But we shouldn't get ahead of ourselves. We should build general theories where the data support them. The "capstone" gambit pushes us to look for generality when it is not there.

SO WHAT DOES it mean to think like a lawyer? It is literalism and formalism, and originalism and instrumentalism, and reasoned elaboration, and more. It is Keen *and* Handy *and* Foster. How do I know? I have seen actual judges in our legal system use those methods. The parishioner who is asked if he believes in baptism replies, "Of course I do, I've seen it done."

Tatting wants to know which method is *the* right one. What criteria would he use to decide? Would he choose the method that maximizes utility? Or promotes liberty? Or promotes Rawls's two principles of justice? Or is there a method inherent in the concept of law or language? And how would he decide among those "meta" criteria?

Maybe we should just be sociologists. I can "observe" the American legal system and describe pretty well what it means to think like a lawyer, just like I can watch a baseball game and describe (pretty well) what it means to follow the rules. If I do that, I can see that arguing that my sister should win because she is my sister is not a "legal" argument. Referring to the literal words, or purposes, or consequences for society is. We might still have disagreements at the margins. Fuller shows us that we can "read" *any* data purely neutrally, so we will have disagreements describing our legal practices. But we can come to a lot of agreement.

PHILIP BOBBITT HAS examined the various modes of legal reasoning in *Constitutional Fate.*[4] Bobbitt focuses on constitutional interpretation, but his conclusions have broader applications. Most jurisprudential scholars focus on what they would *like* to see as judicial methodology. Bobbitt surveys actual cases in our legal culture and catalogs the different ways judges interpret legal materials. He brackets his values and just tries to describe the data. We may not be able to do this fully, but we can try. It is much like Ernest Hemingway trying to describe the phenomenon of bacon frying without trying to put it into a cultural context.

Under Bobbitt's approach, the role of a first-year law teacher would be to make students understand the various methods that are acceptable in our legal system. We might step outside of our practices and evaluate them, just as we might do for substantive legal rules. But the ultimate arbiter would be to ascertain with a cold eye what the actual methods of our legal system are, just as we do for substantive legal rules. We might like them or not, and we can certainly evaluate them from some normative perspective, but whether they are part of thinking like a lawyer depends on widespread usages in our actual legal practices.

Bobbitt identifies six modes: literal, structural, historical, doctrinal, prudential, and ethical.[5] The *literal* approach has a judge look to words in their everyday meaning, much like Keen. The *structural* mode looks to the structure of the relevant unit of the government or the relationships between structures if more than one unit is relevant. Think here of Brandeis's argument in *Erie,* which rests on the relation of federal courts to state law in cases in which a citizen of one state sues a citizen of another.[6] The *historical* mode uses legislative history to determine the meaning of a statute or constitutional provision, and the *doctrinal* mode appeals to principles established in precedents or expounded in authoritative treatises. *Prudential* arguments are based on the consequences of a particular ruling. Would a rule make it difficult for courts to try cases or for the police to do their job? An *ethical* argument does not invoke the judge's own ethical views, but it refers to the "ethos" of our culture. It is much like Hart and Sacks's use of reasoned elaboration or Dworkin's reference to our deep cultural values. The point is not to rehearse all of Bobbitt's points. It is to focus on his methodology of using actual legal practice to ascertain what it means to think like a lawyer.

Bobbitt's approach is descriptive. Nonetheless, for the same reasons on which Lon Fuller based his attack on the positivists, Bobbitt can't be entirely descriptive. We can find a few individual judges who use fringe methods. Justice Oscar Mauzy in Texas once famously decided a case by stating that the votes had changed on the Texas Supreme Court. Raw politics seems to have been his method. Bobbitt does not include that as a mode—and rightly so. But the process of excluding fringe cases from a description involves some normative judgments.

Nevertheless, Bobbitt is at least *largely* descriptive and tries as best he can to avoid normative judgments.

THIS APPROACH SETS an attractive agenda for legal education. First-year students are trying to learn how to become lawyers in *our* particular legal system. Why not teach them the prevailing methods? This doesn't mean we can't have opinions about the method from a normative point of view any more than we can't have opinions about the tax code. But students ought to know what those methods are, just as they ought to know the content of particular areas of law.

This approach also is attractive philosophically. Philosophy ought to clarify and make sense of intellectual practices. The philosophy of science, for example, should make the best account it can of scientific reasoning. Do electrons really exist? Or are they just useful fictions devised to help us make predictions? The answer ought to be what gives us the best understanding of how science works. Indeed, Albert Einstein and Niels Bohr had just this philosophical debate arising out of the Copenhagen interpretation of quantum mechanics.

Shouldn't the same be true of legal philosophy? Is "literalism" an appropriate legal method? Of course it is. I have seen it done. We can be positivistic about legal reasoning in just the same way that we can be positivistic about the content of tort law. Even if I don't like an aspect of tort law, it is still law. Even if I don't like a jurisprudential decision-making method, it still is one in our legal system. Isn't that what Austin was trying to do?

THERE IS NO algorithm for a judge to decide which method is the right one or the right one to use in a particular case. Sometimes this will mean that the outcome of a case is indeterminate. That was Tatting's problem. Bobbitt's methodological polytheism is just another degree of freedom for a judge.

Sometimes law itself provides an answer to the question of method. In contract cases, the plain meaning rule provides that a judge can go beyond the clear words of a contract only to resolve ambiguity in the words themselves. The judge cannot use extra contractual material to create ambiguity. Article 2 of the Uniform Commercial Code says judges should consider trade usage and course of dealing. But in most cases the *law* does not provide an answer to the question of method. So a judge is free to select one. Different methods often lead to different results, so the judge seems to have the freedom to reach the results he wants. What happened to the rule of law?

First-year law students fall into one of two camps. Some are frustrated anytime a particular legal method reaches an unjust or unfair result, so they are happy to have the freedom to back any result they want. But a more common reaction is that they want law to produce a definitive answer. This may be due as much to anxiety about exams as to jurisprudential angst, but for whatever reason they want to know "the" answer. Students complain that professors "hide the ball" on questions of substantive law. Now they seem to hide the ball on methodology. Or worse yet: each professor has her own preferred method, so the ground rules change from class to class.

Bobbitt's approach, at least, is honest. We may wish for a more determinate approach, but if our task is to teach about the world as it actually is, not as we wish it to be, then methodological polytheism appears to be a "fact" of our legal world. So one answer to this frustration is: "Sorry, that's just the way the world is."

But the "problem" of indeterminacy is not as bad as it appears. These sources of indeterminacy do not occur in every case. In most cases, we agree on the method and the substantive answer. That does not appear in Supreme Court cases, but those are hardly a random sample. Ninety-nine people out of a hundred will conclude that a baby buggy is not a vehicle to be banned from the park, and they will do so because they understand the purpose of the ordinance. We know what the law means most of the time. That is what allows us to plan our lives in a way that we can be more productive and be secure in our rights to liberty and property. The world does not have to be entirely predictable to make it be predictable enough. We can embrace all of these methods and still predict with a great deal of certainty the outcome of most cases most of the time.

We might actually conduct an experiment. Suppose we take a thousand randomly selected legal questions. We can't select only Supreme Court cases, or even cases that come before a court. They are a skewed sample. Most legal questions never get to court. I might ask myself whether I can help myself to the food in my neighbor's refrigerator. That is an easy case. I know that I cannot because my neighbor "owns" it. So we take a thousand randomly selected legal questions, and two groups of people predict how a court would decide. They try to give the "correct" legal answer. One group is trained in legal analysis; they might have been to law school. The other is simply asked to predict what a judge would do based on the judge's political affiliation. There will be more agreement among the legally trained group. Law and a shared understanding of legal reasoning effectively give order to the world.

Lawyers will come to agreement in many or most cases because we share an interpretive culture, not because there is an intrinsically right answer. As we saw, equality doesn't intrinsically mean equality of opportunity, but at one time we "knew" that it did. As Balkin would say, we "privileged" one view of equality as a shared convention. At one time, equality did not include sexual orientation. Now it does. There is no intrinsic reason that we read Blake's "London" broadly rather than narrowly, but we share an interpretive convention to read poetry metaphorically.

Different modes of legal reasoning serve as reminders. In poetry, a critic who jumps immediately to social context can overlook nuances in language that a literalist would see—and vice versa. Or we can overlook hints at meaning by failing to appreciate structure. If judges would at least consider each mode, they might glean hints of interpretation that they otherwise would overlook. Considering the different modes would give them an opportunity at least to reduce the size of H. L. A. Hart's penumbra.

There are still cases in which we are left with an existential choice. Bobbitt calls this "conscience." Realists called it "psychology" or "politics." But a judge's path to get to that point might exhaust all of the modes of analysis, and they might coalesce into a more definitive answer. If judges are lazy, or don't act in good faith, they can jump immediately to politics, but they don't have to.

HART AND SACKS have a wonderful case in *The Legal Process* to highlight the sin of judicial laziness or bad faith. Recall the *Case of the Burnt Bundles.*[7] Did a railroad's obligation end when it delivered goods to the platform—as does a ship's—or only when it delivers the goods to the shipper—as does a buggy's? The court could easily have just distinguished railroads from ships *and* buggies and decided however it wanted. But the court wasn't lazy or acting in bad faith. It *tried* to find the "best" answer by using reasoned elaboration. In this context, a railroad is more like a ship than a buggy.

The very next case Hart and Sacks take up in *The Legal Process* is *Berenson v. Nirenstein.*[8] The judge in this case, Judge C. J. Qua, had to decide whether a promise not in writing was enforceable. Like the case of the burnt bundles, there were two lines of cases. One, which would not enforce the promise, was based on the statute of frauds. The other, which would enforce it, was based on constructive trust. Judge Qua just distinguished the case from the cases in the first line on factual grounds and then enforced the promise. But the cases in the second line were also distinguishable. Qua stopped too early. He was lazy or disingenuous. So plainly, there are theoretical places where judges have "discretion." But hard work and good faith can reduce them as a practical matter.

WE WILL COME TO more agreement when we apply these modes of reasoning in areas or eras where we share common values and assumptions. It was easier for Hart and Sacks to think we could come to agreement in the mid-twentieth century. The Vietnam War changed all that. It is even worse today when we live in our own echo chambers. That is a pernicious problem in itself. It has the added pernicious consequence of splintering our shared interpretational conventions. And it fosters bad faith. But it should not be surprising to learn that law doesn't work as well in a fractured society. Law can solve some of our problems, but it can't solve them all.

In any event, why would we want law to act like a determinative algorithm? I often ask students, "Wouldn't it be a shame if the law was a deterministic algorithm?" Their generation would have nothing to add (except, of course, in legislation). Some level of indeterminacy gives each generation the flexibility to carve out its own future. So, unquestionably, there is some indeterminacy in law. But so what? Maybe the indeterminacy we have in law is just the right combination of order and predictability, on the one hand, and flexibility and creativity on the other. In any event, so be it. The point here is to understand the system we have.

THIS BRINGS US BACK to legal education. Law schools are supposed to be where lawyers learn about shared conventions of interpretation, where they learn to think like lawyers. But we spend less time on that than we used to. We care about coverage and use multiple-choice exams. We care more about results—and how they fit our own ideas about justice—than we do about process. Fewer students take "process" courses or "perspectives" courses such as federal courts, conflict of laws, legal history, and legal philosophy. Hart and Sacks are old-fashioned and even reactionary. It is naïve to think that we can trust the process of law or legal reasoning to reach (minimally) acceptable results. At a colloquium some years ago, where the presenter did focus on process and methodology, the overwhelming reaction was that the proposed process couldn't be right because it reached the wrong result. We simply don't work very hard on having our students learn about the process of law as a social institution or to learn about legal reasoning. We care more about justice.

When we do focus on method, we are often cynical. It is always more fun to point out the costs of formalism in an individual case than to show its systematic benefits. It is easier to champion the Handsome Sailor than John Claggart. It is fun pulling back the curtain to show that the Wizard is just an old man. Shouldn't we spend a bit more time getting students to focus on how the system works?

The centrifugal forces in our society are strong. Shouldn't law, and law school, add some centripetal force, not by agreeing on what justice consists of but instead by studying moderately shared modes of reasoning? In "The Second Coming," William Butler Yeats tells us:

Turning and turning in the widening gyre
The falcon cannot hear the falconer;
Things fall apart; the center cannot hold;
Mere anarchy is loosed upon the world,
The blood-dimmed tide is loosed, and everywhere
The ceremony of innocence is drowned;
The best lack all conviction, while the worst
Are full of passionate intensity.

Surely some revelation is at hand;
Surely the Second Coming is at hand.
The Second Coming! Hardly are those words out
When a vast image out of Spiritus Mundi
Troubles my sight: somewhere in sands of the desert
A shape with lion body and the head of a man,
A gaze blank and pitiless as the sun,
Is moving its slow thighs, while all about it
Reel shadows of the indignant desert birds.
The darkness drops again; but now I know
That twenty centuries of stony sleep
Were vexed to nightmare by a rocking cradle,
And what rough beast, its hour come round at last,
Slouches towards Bethlehem to be born?[9]

This is a cautionary tale.

And there is a serendipitous message. We don't have to choose sharply between process and justice. Hart and Sacks would have us look at a law's purposes to help determine what it means. This is one aspect of thinking like a lawyer that tends to inculcate civic values and a sensitivity to social justice. It helps guard against blind obedience and callousness. Systematic examination of the purposes of accounting rules in business school might have helped prevent the Enron Corporation scandal.

LET US RETURN to the first year of law school and finish with how a polytheistic approach to legal reasoning might work in a problem many first-year torts courses start with. In *Ghassemieh v. Schafer,* a junior high school art teacher, Karen Ghassemieh, had a chair pulled out from under her by a student, Elaine Schafer, as she was sitting down. [10] The teacher fell to the floor and hurt her back. She sued Schafer for negligence in causing her injury. The problem was that Schafer, as she testified at trial, had intentionally pulled the chair away "as a joke." She had, in other words, intentionally caused Ghassemieh to fall to the floor, and since her act had resulted in Ghassemieh's hurting her back, she therefore appeared to be liable for battery. But could she be liable for battery if she were also liable for negligence and vice versa? And if not, did that mean that Ghassemieh, because she had sued for negligence, loses if the jury determines that she was the victim of a battery?

That is in fact what happened, and Ghassemieh then appealed. The question before the appellate court was whether Schafer's act could be a battery if she didn't, as she also testified, intend to harm Ghassemieh. The court held that the question turned not on whether Schafer had intended to harm Ghassemieh but rather on whether she had acted without Ghassemieh's consent. A battery is an intentional touching of another, either directly or indirectly, which is harmful or offensive. The court, following a decision in a previous case in which a child pulled a similar prank, declared "the intent to do harm is not essential to a battery."[11] Consequently, an action like Schafer's can be a battery and at the same time exhibit negligence if the harm it causes, despite being unintentional, is foreseeable. Ghassemieh, having staked her claim to a reversible error in the trial judge's having instructed the jury about Schafer's not having committed a battery, lost her appeal.

The appellate court reached its conclusion by interpreting the common law definition of battery literally, finding support for this interpretation in the earlier case and in authoritative treatises. In taking the intent to do harm as inessential to battery, the court accepted the view common to opinions in past cases that the duty breached in a battery is the duty not to touch someone. The breach, then, on this view, is a basis for a suit when the person touched is harmed, and because consent to being touched negates the duty, the full definition of battery includes, as an element, absence of consent.

The definition, however, is open to a different interpretation if, using the method of reasoned elaboration, one asks what the law's purpose is in making absence of consent an element of the definition. Is it to protect an interest in not being touched? Or is it to protect an interest in not being harmed as a consequence of being touched? Given a culture in which people freely touch one another in benign ways—a tap on the shoulder to get someone's attention, a spontaneous hug or clasping of another's hand to show sympathy, a clap on the back to express congratulations—it makes little sense to see the law's purpose as protecting an interest in not being touched. After all, we would not ordinarily think you breach a duty when, on a crowded bus or subway, you press against the person seated next to you to make room for another passenger. So the method of reasoned elaboration yields an interpretation of the definition as requiring not only an intent to touch but also an intent to harm as a consequence of touching. It yields an interpretation contrary to the one the court in *Ghassemieh* gave.

So contrary interpretations of the common law definition of battery can flow from different judicial outlooks and their correlative modes of legal reasoning. One mode emphasizes respect for decisions in prior cases and the stability it brings. Another regards the law in light of the values its purpose is to promote and seeks progress in their pursuit. The pervasive yin and yang of social thought is inherent too in the life of the law.

WE HAVE SURVEYED the contours of thinking like a lawyer—and the process of legal education surrounding it. Much is still up for grabs. There are many loose ends. Justices Keen, Handy, and Foster (and Tatting) probably still disagree. There is no single way to think like a lawyer.

So, we return to where we started. Law students, and citizens interested in the selection of judges, should at least understand the backstories behind these debates. They should attend finishing school about our legal culture. Then they can make up their own minds.

Hopefully, now they have. And they can.

Notes

CHAPTER 1: "I WANT MY OLD MIND BACK"

1. Edwin W. Patterson, *The Case Method in American Legal Education: Its Origins and Objectives*, 4 J. LEGAL EDUC. 1, 2–3 (1951).

2. *See* Alan A. Stone, *Legal Education on the Couch*, 85 HARV. L. REV. 392, 398–401 (1971) (discussing the lack of commitments required of a typical first-year law student prior to commencing their legal education, resulting in a prolonged period of uncertainty about various facets of their identity, including professional, personal, and ideological).

3. *See* Oliver Wendell Holmes, Brown University—Commencement 1897, *in* COLLECTED LEGAL PAPERS 164, 164–65 (1920) (acknowledging Edmund Burke's assertion).

4. Sam Hurt, "Fish Law," Eyebeam.

5. JOHN RAWLS, A THEORY OF JUSTICE 235 (Harvard Univ. Press 1971).

6. *Id.* at 239–40.

7. *See* LON L. FULLER, THE MORALITY OF LAW (Yale Univ. Press rev. ed. 1969), 152–86.

8. Focus on ordinary cases in private law, and not the great cases of constitutional controversy, for theorizing about legal reasoning was the hallmark of the Legal Process School. See pp. 107–108.

9. See chapter 4 (pp. 66–82 for entire chapter).

10. For discussions of scholars who do so, *see, e.g.*, Gerald Turkel, *Michel Foucault: Law, Power, and Knowledge*, 17 J.L. & SOC'Y 170, 178–87 (1990), and Michael Clarke, *Durkheim's Sociology of Law*, 3 BRIT. J.L. & SOC'Y 246, 246–51 (1976).

11. *See, e.g.*, FULLER, THE MORALITY OF LAW, 152–86.

12. RAWLS, A THEORY OF JUSTICE, 260–63.

13. PLATO, REPUBLIC 514a–16c (G. M. A. Grube trans., rev. by C. D. C. Reeve 1992).

14. *See generally* Guido Calabresi & A. Douglas Melamed, *Property Rules, Liability Rules, and Inalienability: One View of the Cathedral*, 85 HARV. L. REV. 1089, 1090 n.2 (1972).

CHAPTER 2: "THE CASE OF THE SPELUNCEAN EXPLORERS"

1. SANFORD LEVINSON, CONSTITUTIONAL FAITH (Princeton Univ. Press 2nd ed. 2011), 29 ("There are . . . two separate variables for each of what I have labeled the 'catholic' and 'protestant' positions. [T]he protestant position is that it is the constitutional text alone (A), while the catholic

position is that the source of doctrine is the text of the Constitution plus unwritten tradition (B).").

2. Lon Fuller, *The Case of the Speluncean Explorers,* 62 HARV. L. REV. 616 (1949).

3. *Id.* at 619.

4. *Id.*

5. *Id.* at 632.

6. *Id.* at 637.

7. *Id.* at 637–38.

8. *Id.* at 638.

9. *Id.* at 620.

10. *Id.* at 621.

11. *Id.* at 625.

12. *Id.* at 635.

13. WILLIAM SHAKESPEARE, OTHELLO, act 1, sc. 3, line 143–44 ("And of the cannibals that each other eat, The Anthropophagi. . . .").

14. FULLER, THE MORALITY OF LAW, 634.

15. *Id.* at 645.

16. *See* William C. Powers Jr., *Formalism and Nonformalism in Choice of Law Methodology,* 52 WASH. L. REV. 27, 28 (1976) ("A formal decision uses less than all available relevant information by following a rule which screens from the decisionmaker's consideration all information not specifically invoked by the rule."); William C. Powers Jr., *Structural Aspects of the Impact of Law on Moral Duty Within Utilitarianism and Social Contract Theory,* 26 UCLA L. REV. 1263, 1268 (1979).

17. *See generally* Duncan Kennedy, *Form and Substance in Private Law Adjudication,* 89 HARV. L. REV. 1685 (1976) (discussing the nature and interconnection of the different rhetorical modes found in American private law opinions, articles, and treatises).

18. LEWIS CARROLL, THROUGH THE LOOKING-GLASS, AND WHAT ALICE FOUND THERE 124 (Avenel Books 1970 [1871]) ("'When *I* use a word,' Humpty Dumpty said in a rather scornful tone, 'it means just what I choose it to mean—neither more nor less.'").

CHAPTER 3: LAW'S CONTOURS

1. *See* Powers, *Structural Aspects,* 1264–65; *see also* Powers, *Formalism,* 27.

2. FRANZ KAFKA, THE TRIAL 326–35 (E. M. Butler ed., Willa & Edwin Muir trans., Random House rev. ed. 1956 [1925]).

3. *See generally* Powers, *Formalism,* at 27 (discussing three structural models of the impact of law on moral duty). *See also* Powers, *Structural Aspects.*

4. John Voland, *Turner Defends Move to Colorize Films*, L.A. TIMES (Oct. 23, 1986), www.latimes.com/archives/la-xpm-1986-10-23-ca-6941-story.html.

5. *See, e.g.*, R. DUNCAN LUCE & HOWARD RAIFFA, GAMES AND DECISIONS: INTRODUCTION AND CRITICAL SURVEY 94–97 (Wiley 1957); PETER C. ORDESHOOK, GAME THEORY AND POLITICAL THEORY: AN INTRODUCTION 206–10 (Cambridge Books 1986).

6. *See generally* JEAN-JACQUES ROUSSEAU, EMILE, OR EDUCATION 84–85 (Barbara Fox trans., J. M. Dent & Sons 4th ed. 1921 [1762]) (tasking the young educator with the crucial "art of controlling without precepts, and doing everything without doing anything at all").

7. V. I. LENIN, THE STATE AND REVOLUTION 16–21 (Robert Service trans., Penguin Books 1992).

8. Alf Ross, *Tû-Tû*, 70 HARV. L. REV. 812 (1957).

9. JEAN-JACQUES ROUSSEAU, THE SOCIAL CONTRACT & DISCOURSES 32–34 (G. D. H. Cole trans., E. P. Dutton & Co. 1950 [1762]).

10. MacPherson v. Buick Motor Co. 111 N.E. 1050 (N.Y. 1916).

11. Winterbottom v. Wright 152 Eng. Rep. 402 (Ex. 1842).

12. Jean-Paul Sartre, *Existentialism Is a Humanism*, in EXISTENTIALISM FROM DOSTOEVSKY TO SARTRE 287, 292–94 (Walter Kaufmann ed. & trans., World Pub. Company 20th ed. 1964 [1956]).

13. *See* FRIEDRICH NIETZSCHE, *The Birth of Tragedy from the Spirit of Music*, *in* THE BIRTH OF TRAGEDY AND THE GENEALOGY OF MORALS 19–23 (F. Golffing trans., 1956) (discussing the Appollonian and Dionysian duality).

14. HERMAN MELVILLE, BILLY BUDD, SAILOR 101 (H. Hayford & M. Sealts eds., Univ. of Chicago Press 1962).

15. *Id.* at 110–11.

16. Shaw, while sitting as the Chief Justice of the Massachusetts Supreme Court from 1830 to 1860, wrote some of the most important judicial opinions, including seminal torts opinions. *See, e.g.*, Brown v. Kendall, 60 Mass. (6 Cush.) 292 (1850) (requiring plaintiff to meet a negligence standard in a trespass action). While Shaw's decisions helped to formulate many areas of law and aided the economic development characteristic of the era, they often did not serve those members of the commonwealth most in need of the law's protection. *See* MORTON J. HORWITZ, THE TRANSFORMATION OF AMERICAN LAW, 1780–1860 at 99 (Harvard Univ. Press 1977). ("The law of negligence became a leading means by which the dynamic and growing forces in American society were able to challenge and eventually overwhelm the weak and relatively powerless segments of the American economy.").

17. *See* ROBERT COVER, JUSTICE ACCUSED: ANTISLAVERY AND THE JUDICIAL PROCESS 4–5 (Yale Univ. Press 1975) (discussing the dichotomy

between Shaw's reputation as a noted, strong opponent to slavery and his judicial decisions that came down hard on fugitive slaves through an unflinching application of the law).

18. *Id.*

19. *See* NIETZSCHE, THE BIRTH OF TRAGEDY.

20. *See* MELVILLE, BILLY BUDD, 129.

21. NIETZSCHE, THE BIRTH OF TRAGEDY, at 19.

22. ALFRED KAZIN, THE PORTABLE BLAKE 46 (Penguin Books ed. 1976 [1946]).

23. JAMES FENIMORE COOPER, THE PIONEERS 15–29 (Penguin Books 1988 [1823]).

24. DIRTY HARRY (Warner Bros. 1971).

25. APOCALYPSE NOW (Zoetrope Studios 1979).

26. JOSEPH CONRAD, HEART OF DARKNESS (Penguin Books 1976 [1902]).

27. APOCALYPSE NOW.

28. GEORGE ORWELL, 1984 (Harcourt, Brace ed. 1949).

29. BORIS PASTERNAK, DOCTOR ZHIVAGO (Richard Pevear & Larissa Volokhonsky trans., Vintage International ed. 2010).

30. LEO TOLSTOY, WAR AND PEACE 1308 (Rosemary Edmonds trans., Penguin Books ed. 1982 [1869]).

31. ALBERT CAMUS, *The Artist at Work, in* EXILE AND THE KINGDOM 110 (Justin O'Brien trans., Knopf ed. 1958).

32. THE EPIC OF GILGAMESH (Andrew George trans., Penguin Books ed. 1999).

33. WALKER PERCY, THE MOVIEGOER (Vintage International ed. 1998).

34. *Id.* at 184–200.

35. SOPHOCLES, OEDIPUS REX (Stephen Berg & Diskin Clay trans., Oxford Univ. Press 1978 [440 BCE]).

CHAPTER 4: LAW AND MORALS

1. Contemporary accounts of positivism distinguish between weaker and stronger conceptions of the separability of law and morality that the school defends. On the weaker conceptions, moral standards as such can be incorporated into law through the practices of judges and other legal officials. For example, the Supreme Court's adoption of "evolving standards of decency," as a test for when punishment is cruel and unusual and therefore a violation of the Eighth Amendment's prohibition on such punishments, makes moral standards part of the law to the extent that judges use this test. *See* Trop v. Dulles 356 U.S. 86 (1958). In this example, the separation is located in the standards' having the force of law by virtue of judicial practice and not by virtue of their being true or valid standards of morality. On stronger conceptions, moral standards are not as such

incorporated into the law when they are adopted by courts as tests for interpreting a statute or constitutional provision, any more than moral precepts forbidding specific conduct (e.g., vandalism) do not become part of the law as a result of a legislature's enacting a law prohibiting the very same conduct. In either case, the legal standards and the moral standards are distinct though they have the same content.—Ed.

2. B. F. SKINNER, ABOUT BEHAVIORISM 9–20 (Knopf 1974).

3. Oliver Wendell Holmes Jr., *The Path of the Law,* 10 HARV. L. REV. 457 (1897).

4. JOHN FINNIS, NATURAL LAW AND NATURAL RIGHTS 23–25 (Oxford Univ. Press 1980).

5. MATTHEW LEVERING, BIBLICAL NATURAL LAW: A THEOCENTRIC AND TELEOLOGICAL APPROACH (Oxford Univ. Press 2008).

6. Jacobellis v. Ohio 378 U.S. 184 (1964), 197.

7. H. L. A. Hart, *Positivism and the Separation of Law and Morals,* 71 HARV. L. REV. 593 (1958).

8. FINNIS, NATURAL LAW AND NATURAL RIGHTS, 59–99.

9. *Id.*

10. RONALD DWORKIN, JUSTICE FOR HEDGEHOGS 405–15 (Harvard Univ. Press 2011).

11. CICERO, ON THE COMMONWEALTH AND ON THE LAWS (J. E. G. Zetzel ed., Cambridge Univ. Press ed. 1999).

12. EPICTETUS, HANDBOOK (Nicholas White trans., Hackett 1983).

13. RICHARD HOOKER, OF THE LAWS OF ECCLESIASTICAL POLITY (A. S. McGrade ed., Cambridge Univ. Press ed. 1989).

14. HUGO GROTIUS, ON THE LAW OF WAR AND PEACE (F. W. Kelsey trans., Oxford Univ. Press ed. 1925).

15. SAMUEL PUFENDORF, ON THE DUTY OF MAN AND CITIZEN ACCORDING TO THE LAW OF NATURE (James Tully ed., Cambridge Univ. Press ed. 1991).

16. JOHN LOCKE, SECOND TREATISE OF GOVERNMENT (C. B. Macpherson ed., Hackett ed. 1980 [1690]).

17. THOMAS AQUINAS, TREATISE ON LAW (Richard J. Regan trans., Hackett ed. 2000).

18. WILLIAM BLACKSTONE, COMMENTARIES ON THE LAWS OF ENGLAND 1, 38–63 (Univ. of Chicago Press facsimile ed. 1979 [1765]).

19. DECLARATION OF INDEPENDENCE para. 2 (U.S. 1776).

20. Martin Luther King Jr., "Letter from Birmingham Jail," in WHY WE CAN'T WAIT 77 (Harper & Row 1963).

21. BLACKSTONE, COMMENTARIES, 42–43.

22. PLATO, REPUBLIC 338c.

23. JEREMY BENTHAM, A FRAGMENT ON GOVERNMENT (J. H. Burns and H. L. A. Hart eds., Cambridge Univ. Press 1988 [1776]).

24. BLACKSTONE, COMMENTARIES, 120–21.

25. DECLARATION OF INDEPENDENCE para. 2.

26. THOMAS HOBBES, LEVIATHAN 86–121 (Richard Tuck ed., Cambridge Univ. Press 1996 [1651]).

27. BENTHAM, OF LAWS IN GENERAL 1 (H. L. A. Hart ed., Althone Press 1970).

28. *Id.* at 18.

29. JOHN AUSTIN, THE PROVINCE OF JURISPRUDENCE DETERMINED (Wilfrid E. Rumble ed., Cambridge Univ. Press 1995 [1832]).

30. *Id.* at 19.

31. *Id.* at 25.

32. *Id.* at 166.

33. Holmes, *The Path of the Law,* 73.

34. HANS KELSEN, PURE THEORY OF LAW (M. Knight trans., Univ. of California Press 1967). The work was originally published in German with the title REINE RECHTSLEHRE, and an expanded second edition was published in 1960.

35. *Id.* at 7–8.

36. *Id.* at 8.

37. *Id.* at 211–12.

38. BENTHAM, OF LAWS IN GENERAL, 18.

39. AUSTIN, THE PROVINCE OF JURISPRUDENCE DETERMINED, 166.

40. HART, THE CONCEPT OF LAW (Oxford Univ. Press 1961).

41. H. L. A. Hart, *Positivism and the Separation of Law and Morals.*

42. Lon Fuller, *Positivism and Fidelity to Law—A Reply to Professor Hart,* 71 HARV. L. REV. 630 (1957).

43. H. L. A. HART, THE CONCEPT OF LAW, 27–28.

44. *Id.* at 49–76.

45. *Id.* at 105–07.

46. *Id.* at 89–96.

47. *Id.* at 92–93 and 102–04.

48. *Id.* at 105–06.

49. Hart, *Positivism and the Separation of Law and Morals,* 619–20. The objector to positivism to whom Hart is responding is Gustav Radbruch, a former adherent to positivism who came to reject it from his experience of the abuses of the German law by the Nazis during the Third Reich.—Ed.

50. *Id.*

51. Fuller, *Positivism and Fidelity to Law,* 652–54.

52. LON FULLER, THE MORALITY OF LAW.

53. Fuller, *Positivism and Fidelity to Law.*

54. *Id.* at 645–46 and FULLER, THE MORALITY OF LAW, 41–44.

55. FULLER, THE MORALITY OF LAW, 41–42.

56. *Id.* at 42.

57. HART, THE CONCEPT OF LAW, 199.

58. FULLER, THE MORALITY OF LAW, 42–43.

59. *Id.* at 133–45.

60. LUDWIG WITTGENSTEIN, PHILOSOPHICAL INVESTIGATIONS (G. E. M. Anscombe trans., Macmillan 1953).

61. Fuller, *Positivism and Fidelity to Law,* 662–63.

62. LUDWIG WITTGENSTEIN, TRACTATUS LOGICO-PHILOSOPHICUS (D. F. Pears & B. F. McGuinness trans., Routledge and Kegan Paul 1961 [1921]).

63. WITTGENSTEIN, PHILOSOPHICAL INVESTIGATIONS.

64. *See* Robert Cooter & Melvin Aron Eisenberg, *Damages for Breach of Contract,* 73 CAL. L. REV. 1438–44 (1985).

65. LON L. FULLER, BASIC CONTRACT LAW (West Publishing 1947). The second edition was published in 1964, with Robert Braucher as coeditor.

66. The divergence between how to begin a contracts casebook purportedly began between Arthur Corbin and Fuller, when the pedagogical rift led to the dissolution of their agreement to coauthor a casebook. Scott D. Gerber, *Corbin and Fuller's Cases on Contract (1942): The Casebook that Never Was,* 72 FORDHAM L. REV. 595 (2003).

67. *See* William N. Eskridge Jr. & Philip P. Frickey, *The Making of the Legal Process,* 107 HARV. L. REV. 2031, 2038–49 (1993).

68. FULLER, THE MORALITY OF LAW, 137–45.

CHAPTER 5: HISTORICAL SCHOOLS OF THOUGHT

1. KARL LLEWELLYN, THE COMMON LAW TRADITION: DECIDING APPEALS (Quid Pro Books 2016 [1960]).

2. GRANT GILMORE, THE AGES OF AMERICAN LAW 108 (Yale Univ. Press ed. 2015 [1977]).

3. *See, e.g.,* HORWITZ, TRANSFORMATION, 1780–1860; *see also* MORTON HORWITZ, THE TRANSFORMATION OF AMERICAN LAW, 1870–1960: THE CRISIS OF LEGAL ORTHODOXY (Oxford Univ. Press 1992).

4. *See, e.g.,* Robert W. Gordon, *Critical Legal Histories,* 36 STAN. L. REV. 57 (1984).

5. *See, e.g.,* Robert M. Cover, *The Supreme Court 1982 Term,* 97 HARV. L. REV. 4 (1983).

6. *See, e.g.,* DAVID M. RABBAN, LAW'S HISTORY: AMERICAN LEGAL THOUGHT AND THE TRANSATLANTIC TURN TO HISTORY (Cambridge Univ. Press 2012).

7. PLATO, CRATYLUS 402a. Fragment 91, Diels-Kranz (HERMANN ALEXANDER DIELS & WALTHER KRANZ, THE FRAGMENTS OF THE PRE-SOCRATICS, 5TH ED.).

8. W. K. C. GUTHRIE, A HISTORY OF GREEK PHILOSOPHY, VOLUME II: THE PRESOCRATIC TRADITION FROM PARMENIDES TO DEMOCRITUS 4–5 (Cambridge Univ. Press 1979).

9. *See* ARISTOTLE, PHYSICS 239b; *see also* PLATO, PARMENIDES 127d–28e.

10. PLATO, CRATYLUS 439a–40d.

11. KARL MARX & FREDERICK ENGELS, MARX & ENGELS COLLECTED WORKS, VOLUME 5: MARX AND ENGELS, 1845–1847 at 409–14 (Lawrence & Wishart 1976).

12. *See, e.g.*, G. A. COHEN, KARL MARX'S THEORY OF HISTORY: A DEFENCE (Princeton Univ. Press 1978); ERIK OLIN WRIGHT, ANDREW LEVINE & ELLIOT SOBER, RECONSTRUCTING MARXISM: ESSAYS ON EXPLANATION AND THEORY OF HISTORY (Verso 1992); NIKOLAUS LOBKOWICZ, THEORY AND PRACTICE: HISTORY OF A CONCEPT FROM ARISTOTLE TO MARX (Univ. of Notre Dame Press 1967); and RICHARD W. MILLER, ANALYZING MARX: MORALITY, POWER, AND HISTORY (Princeton Univ. Press 1984).

13. BLACKSTONE, COMMENTARIES, vols. 1–4.

14. Thomas G. Barnes, *Introduction to Coke's "Commentary on Littleton"* (1995), in LAW, LIBERTY, AND PARLIAMENT: SELECTED ESSAYS ON THE WRITINGS OF SIR EDWARD COKE 1, 24 (Allen D. Boyer ed., Liberty Fund 2004) (discussing Coke's strong influence on colonial law); Roscoe Pound, *The Development of Constitutional Guarantees of Liberty in Medieval England*, 20 NOTRE DAME LAW. 183, 229 (1945) (discussing the influence of Coke's doctrine over that set forth by Blackstone).

15. *See* Henry Monaghan, *Stare Decisis and Constitutional Adjudication*, 88 COLUM. L. REV. 723 (1988) (discussing the importance of America having a *written* Constitution).

16. BLACKSTONE, COMMENTARIES, vol. 1, 327.

17. Slade v. Morley 76 Eng. Rep. 1072 (KB 1602).

18. *See* JAMES BARR AMES, LECTURES ON LEGAL HISTORY, LECTURE 13: EXPRESS ASSUMPSIT 128 (Cambridge 1913) (It is said that "no case has been found recognizing the validity of a promise 'to pay' a precedent debt before 1542"). *But see* Morton Horwitz, *The Historical Foundations of Modern Contract Law*, 87 HARV. L. REV. 917, 919–20, 929–31, 936 (1974) (without stating categorically that executory contracts were never recognized, discusses how they were rarely enforced).

19. HORWITZ, TRANSFORMATION, 1780–1860, at 99.

20. *Id.* at 38–41.

21. *Id.* at 39–42.

22. *Id.* at 93–99.

23. *See* LLEWELLYN, THE COMMON LAW TRADITION, 5, 36–38 (discussing the term's meaning); *see also* GILMORE, THE AGES OF AMERICAN LAW (discussing and elaborating on Llewellyn's use of the phrase).

24. JAMES WILLARD HURST, THE GROWTH OF AMERICAN LAW: THE LAW MAKERS, 183–89 (The Lawbook Exchange ed. 2007 [1950]).

25. Charles River Bridge v. Warren Bridge 36 U.S. (11 Pet.) 420 (1837).

26. Swift v. Tyson 41 U.S. (16 Pet.) 1 (1842).

27. HORWITZ, TRANSFORMATION, 1780–1860, at 88–98.

28. Walton H. Hamilton, *The Ancient Maxim Caveat Emptor,* 40 YALE L.J. 1133, 1156, 1164–66 (1931).

29. HORWITZ, TRANSFORMATION, 1780–1860, at 178–82.

30. *See* Roscoe Pound, *Mechanical Jurisprudence,* 8 COLUM. L. REV. 605, 607, 620–21 (1908) (describing mechanical jurisprudence as the perception that judges have little discretion because the law—not judicial philosophies, ideology, or partisanship—structures courts' decision-making). *See also* HORWITZ, TRANSFORMATION, 1870–1960, at 186–89.

31. Grant Gilmore, *Formalism and the Law of Negotiable Instruments,* 13 CREIGHTON L. REV. 441, 446–48 (1979).

32. HORWITZ, TRANSFORMATION, 1870–1960, at 66–71.

33. *Id.* at 72–75.

34. *Id.* at 38–40.

35. Roscoe Pound, *The Economic Interpretation and the Law of Torts,* 53 HARV. L. REV. 365, 373–79 (1940). *See also* OLIVER WENDELL HOLMES, THE COMMON LAW 16 (Mark DeWolfe Howe ed., Little Brown and Co. 1963 [1881]).

36. HORWITZ, TRANSFORMATION, 1780–1860, at 210–12.

37. ROBERT COVER, JUSTICE ACCUSED: ANTISLAVERY AND THE JUDICIAL PROCESS 151–57 (Yale Univ. Press 1975).

38. *See* CHARLES DICKENS, BLEAK HOUSE (Vintage Classics ed. 2012 [1853]).

39. KARL MARX, THE CIVIL WAR IN FRANCE (Int'l Library Pub. Co. 1900 [1871]).

40. *See generally* WILLIAM E. FORBATH, LAW AND THE SHAPING OF THE AMERICAN LABOR MOVEMENT (1991) (discussing the relationship between the emergence and rise of labor union membership, coordinated organizing, and passage of labor legislation).

41. Morton Horwitz, *Rise of Legal Formalism,* 19 AM. J. LEGAL HIST. 251, 253 (1975).

42. *Id.* at 255–56, 263–64; *see also* Patterson, *The Case Method in American Legal Education.*

43. *See* ROBERT BOCKING STEVENS, LAW SCHOOL: LEGAL EDUCATION IN AMERICA FROM THE 1850S TO THE 1980s, 35–72 (1983). (discussing the "academization" of law schools in the United States).

44. *Id.*

45. *Id.* at 53–64.

46. *See* RESTATEMENT (THIRD) OF TORTS § 29.

47. *Id.* Reporter's Notes to comment a.

48. *Id.* at comment d.

49. HORWITZ, TRANSFORMATION, 1870–1960, at 255–56.

50. *Id.*

51. *See, e.g.,* Pound, *The Economic Interpretation and the Law of Torts,* 615–17; MORRIS COHEN, THE PROCESS OF JUDICIAL LEGISLATION IN

LAW AND THE SOCIAL ORDER (Harcourt, Brace & Co. 1933); T. Alexander Aleinikoff, *Constitutional Law in the Age of Balancing,* 96 YALE L. J. 943 (1987).

52. Holmes, J., *in* Lochner v. New York, 198 U.S. 45, 75 (1905).

53. *Id.* at 76.

54. Holmes, *The Path of the Law.*

55. Lochner v. New York 198 U.S. 45, 76 (1905).

56. *Id.*

57. Riggs v Palmer 115 N.Y. 506, 22 N.E. 188, 191 (1889).

58. *See* Roscoe Pound, *The Need of a Sociological Jurisprudence,* 10 CRIME AND DELINQUENCY 398 (1964); originally published in *The Green Bag,* vol. 19, no. 4, 1907. *See also* Roscoe Pound, *The Scope and Purpose of Sociological Jurisprudence,* 24 HARV. L. REV. 591 (1911); Edward White, *From Sociological Jurisprudence to Realism: Jurisprudence and Social Change in Early Twentieth-Century America,* 58 VA. L. REV. 999 (1972).

59. HORWITZ, TRANSFORMATION, 1870–1960, at 60.

60. Pound, *The Economic Interpretation and the Law of Torts,* 373–81.

61. G. Edward White, *From Sociological Jurisprudence to Realism.*

62. *Id.*

63. Mark V. Tushnet, *Anti-Formalism in Recent Constitutional Theory,* 83 MICH. L. REV. 1502 (1985).

64. *Id.* at 1537–39.

65. DREW PEARSON & ROBERT S. ALLEN, THE NINE OLD MEN (Doubleday, Doran & Co. 1936) (referring to the justices as "nine old men").

66. West Coast Hotel Co. v. Parrish 300 U.S. 379, 400 (1937); NLRB v. Jones & Laughlin Steel Corp. 301 U.S. 1, 43 (1937).

67. Richard D. Friedman, *Switching Time and Other Thought Experiments: The Hughes Court and Constitutional Transformation,* 142 U. PA. L. REV. 1891, 1895–97 (1994).

68. JEROME FRANK, LAW AND THE MODERN MIND (Brentano's 1930).

69. LLEWELLYN, THE COMMON LAW TRADITION.

70. KARL LLEWELLYN, THE BRAMBLE BUSH: ON OUR LAW AND ITS STUDY (Quid Pro ed. 2016 [1930]).

71. *See generally* SAMUEL WILLISTON, LIFE AND LAW (Little, Brown & Co. 1940)

72. UCC § 1–201(3); UCC § 1–303(c).

73. *Id.* § 1–303(c).

74. *Id.* § 1–303(b).

75. LAURA KALMAN, LEGAL REALISM AT YALE, 1927–1960 at 130 (1986); RONEN SHAMIR, MANAGING LEGAL UNCERTAINTY: ELITE LAWYERS IN THE NEW DEAL 131–57 (1995) (chapter 6).

76. Daniel R. Ernst, *Common Laborers-Industrial Pluralists, Legal Realists, and the Law of Industrial Disputes,* 11 LAW & HIST. REV. 59, 66–68, 79–83 (1993).

77. UCC § 2–302, comment 1.

78. 111 N.E. 1050 (N.Y. 1916).

79. 10 M. & W. 109, 152 Eng. Rep. 402 (1842).

80. Thomas v. Winchester 6 N.Y. 397 (1852).

81. Devlin v. Smith 89 N.Y. 470 (1882).

82. Statler v. Ray Mfg. Co. 195 N.Y. 478, 88 N.E. 1063 (1909).

83. Palsgraf v. Long Island R.R. Co. 162 N.E. 99 (N.Y. 1928).

84. William Powers Jr., *Thaumatrope,* 77 TEX. L. REV. 1319, 1329–30 (1999).

85. *In* Re Polemis 3 K.B. 560, 577 [1921] (A.C.) (Eng.).

86. Overseas Tankship (U.K.) Ltd. v Morts Dock & Eng'g Co. (Wagon Mound I), [1961] A.C. 388 (J.C.).

87. Ehrgott v. Mayor 96 N.Y. 264 (1884).

88. 162 N.E. 99, 101 (N.Y. 1928).

89. Powers, *Thaumatrope,* 1320 (discussing Leon S. Lipson, *The Allegheny College Case,* 23 YALE L. REP. 8, 11 (1977)).

90. Lipson, *The Allegheny College Case,* 23 YALE L. REP. 8, 11 (1977).

91. Palsgraf v. Long Island R.R. Co. 162 N.E. 99, 102 (N.Y. 1928) (Andrews, J., dissent).

92. Erie Railroad Co. v. Tompkins 304 U.S. 64 (1938).

93. *Id.* at 102; *see generally,* Henry Friendly, *The Historic Basis of Diversity Jurisdiction,* 41 HARV. L. REV. 483 (1928) (discussing the historical background and development of the federal jurisdiction rule followed in federal court).

94. Swift v. Tyson 41 U.S. (16 Pet.) 1 (1842).

95. Graham Hughes, *Duties to Trespassers: A Comparative Survey and Revaluation,* 68 Yale L.J. 633, 635 (1959).

96. See Judiciary Act of 1789, ch. 20, § 25, I Stat. 73, 85–86. *See also* Charles Warren, *New Light on the History of the Federal Judiciary Act of 1789,* 37 HARV. L. REV. 49, 84–85 (1923).

97. 28 U.S.C. § 2071–77.

98. Erie Railroad Co. v. Tompkins 304 U.S. 64, 79 (1938) (Brandeis was quoting Holmes in Black & White Taxicab & Transfer Co. v. Brown & Yellow Taxicab & Transfer Co. 276 U.S. 518 (1928) dissent at 533.).

CHAPTER 6: HISTORICAL SCHOOLS OF THOUGHT

1. Brown v. Board of Education of Topeka 347 U.S. 483 (1954).

2. United States v. Carroll Towing Co. 159 F.2d 169 (2nd Cir. 1947).

3. Henningsen v. Bloomfield Motors, Inc. 32 N.J. 358, 161 A.2d 69 (1960).

4. U.S. CONST. art. III, § 2.

5. Fairchild v. Hughes 258 U.S. 126 (1922); Massachusetts v. Mellon 262 US 447 (1923).

6. Abbott Laboratories v. Gardner 387 U.S. 136 (1937).

7. Aetna Life Ins. v Haworth 300 U.S. 227 (1937).

8. Baker v. Carr 369 U.S. 186 (1962).

9. HENRY M. HART JR. & HERBERT WECHSLER, THE FEDERAL COURTS AND THE FEDERAL SYSTEM (Foundation Press 1st ed. 1953).

10. HENRY M. HART JR. & ALBERT M. SACKS, THE LEGAL PROCESS: BASIC PROBLEMS IN THE MAKING AND APPLICATION OF LAW 10–68 (William N. Eskridge Jr. & Philip P. Frickey eds., 1994).

11. L. Gillarde Co. v. Joseph Martinelli & Co. 169 F.2d 60 (1st Cir. 1948).

12. Jenkins v. Rose's 5-10-25 Cent Store, Inc. 213 N.C. 606 (1938).

13. Norway Plains Co. v. Bos. & Me. R.R. 67 Mass. 263 (1854).

14. Lichten v. Eastern Airlines, Inc. 189 F.2d 939 (2nd Cir. 1951); HART & SACKS, THE LEGAL PROCESS, 240–65.

15. Youngstown Sheet and Tube Co. v. Sawyer 343 U.S. 579 (1952).

16. Fred Schauer, *Easy Cases,* 58 S. CAL. L. REV. 399 (1985).

17. HART & SACKS, THE LEGAL PROCESS, 10–60.

18. PLATO, REPUBLIC 331c–d.

19. *Id.* at 332a8–b7.

20. *Id.* at 338c1–2.

21. *Id.* at 514a1–517a6.

22. *Id.* 369a1–427e5.

23. Jenkins v. Rose's 5-10-25 Cent Stores, Inc. 213 N.C. 606 (1938).

24. Riggs v. Palmer 115 N.Y. 506, 22 N.E. 188 (1889).

25. HART & SACKS, THE LEGAL PROCESS, 1114, excerpting FRANCIS LIEBER, LEGAL AND POLITICAL HERMENEUTICS, OR PRINCIPLES OF INTERPRETATION AND CONSTRUCTION IN LAW AND POLITICS 18 1837 (William G. Hammond ed., St. Louis, F. H. Thomas & Co. 3rd ed. 1880 [1837]). In Lieber's example, the instruction to the housekeeper is simply "Fetch some soupmeat" accompanied by giving the housekeeper some money. Lieber used the example to point out how much of the instruction is unstated and left to interpretation (e.g., that the money is to be used to purchase the meat and that what is not spent is to be returned).—Ed.

26. Norway Plains Co. v. Bos. & Me. R.R. 67 Mass. 263 (1854). *See* HART & SACKS, THE LEGAL PROCESS, 386–95; *see also Id.* (discussion of *Norway Plains* as Problem No. 11 in chapter 3, section 2).

27. HART & SACKS, THE LEGAL PROCESS, 1133–42.

28. Johnson v. Southern Pacific Co. 117 F. 462 (8th Cir. 1902).

29. Johnson v. Southern Pacific Co. 196 U.S. 1 (1904).

30. WITTGENSTEIN, PHILOSOPHICAL INVESTIGATIONS.

31. HART & SACKS, THE LEGAL PROCESS, 1124.

32. Youngstown Sheet and Tube Co. v. Sawyer 343 U.S. 579 (1952).

33. HART & SACKS, THE LEGAL PROCESS, 457–58.

34. *Id.* at 286–87.

35. *Id.* at 104.

36. *See* pp. 189–90.

37. Ronald Dworkin, *Hard Cases,* 88 HARV. L. REV. 1057 (1975).

38. RONALD DWORKIN, TAKING RIGHTS SERIOUSLY (Harvard Univ. Press 1977); RONALD DWORKIN, A MATTER OF PRINCIPLE (Harvard Univ. Press 1985); RONALD DWORKIN, LAW'S EMPIRE (Harvard Univ. Press 1986); RONALD DWORKIN, JUSTICE IN ROBES (Harvard Univ. Press 2006).

39. Dworkin, *Hard Cases,* 1089–93.

40. Dworkin did not share this aversion. *See* LAW'S EMPIRE, at 355–99.—Ed.

41. Brown v. Board of Education of Topeka 347 U.S. 483 (1954).

42. 381 U.S. 479 (1965).

43. 410 U.S. 113 (1973).

CHAPTER 7: TWO BACKGROUND MORAL THEORIES

1. RAWLS, A THEORY OF JUSTICE, 24–25 and 404–07.

2. *Id.* at 27–33 and 446–52.

3. JEREMY BENTHAM, AN INTRODUCTION TO THE PRINCIPLES OF MORALS AND LEGISLATION (J. H. Burns & H. L. A. Hart eds., Methuen & Co. 1982 [1789]).

4. J. S. MILL, UTILITARIANISM (George Sher ed., Hackett Publishing Co. 1979 [1863]).

5. Many contemporary utilitarians follow Bentham in identifying the good with the happiness of all animals capable of experiencing pleasure and pain.—Ed.

6. *See, e.g.,* DAVID LYONS, FORMS AND LIMITS OF UTILITARIANISM (Oxford Univ. Press 1965); J. J. C. SMART & BERNARD WILLIAMS, UTILITARIANISM: FOR AND AGAINST (Cambridge Univ. Press 1973); AMARTYA SEN & BERNARD WILLIAMS EDS., UTILITARIANISM AND BEYOND (Cambridge Univ. Press 1982); DONALD REGAN, UTILITARIANISM AND COOPERATION (Oxford Univ. Press 1980).

7. See JAMES GRIFFIN, WELL-BEING: ITS MEANING, MEASUREMENT, AND MORAL IMPORTANCE (Oxford Univ. Press 1986).

8. J. S. MILL, UTILITARIANISM.

9. J. S. MILL, ON LIBERTY (E. Rappaport ed., Hackett Publishing Co. 1978 [1859]).

10. Powers, *Structural Aspects of the Impact of Law,* 1276.

11. *Id.*

12. W. S. JEVONS, THE THEORY OF POLITICAL ECONOMY (Macmillan 4th ed. rpt. 1924 [1871]); Lionel Robbins, *Interpersonal Comparisons of Utility: A Comment,* 68 ECON. J. 635 (1938); I. M. D. LITTLE, A CRITIQUE OF WELFARE ECONOMICS (Oxford Univ. Press 2nd ed. 1957); Robert Nozick, *Interpersonal Utility Theory,* 2 Social Choice and Welfare 161 (1985); Marc Fleurbaey & Peter Hammond, *Interpersonally Comparable Utility,* in 2 HANDBOOK OF UTILITY THEORY 1181 (S. Barbera, P. J. Hammond & C. Seidl eds., Kluwer Acad. Pub. 1998).

13. J. M. E. MCTAGGART, THE NATURE OF EXISTENCE, VOLUME 2 (Cambridge Univ. Press 1927) §870. For a more recent treatment, *see* ROGER CRISP, REASONS AND THE GOOD (Oxford Univ. Press 2006), 112.

14. Judith Jarvis Thomson, *The Trolley Problem,* 94 YALE L. J. 1395 (1985). The use of hypotheticals involving a runaway trolley to test one's intuitions about permissible and impermissible killings originated in the work of Philippa Foot. See her *Abortion and the Doctrine of Double Effect,* 5 OXFORD REV. 5 (1967).—Ed.

15. Powers, *Structural Aspects of the Impact of Law;* LIAM B. MURPHY, MORAL DEMANDS IN NONIDEAL THEORY (Oxford Univ. Press 2000).

16. RICHARD BRANDT, A THEORY OF THE RIGHT AND THE GOOD (Clarendon Press 1979), 286–305; BRAD HOOKER, IDEAL CODE, REAL WORLD: A RULE CONSEQUENTIALIST THEORY OF MORALITY (Oxford Univ. Press 2000).

17. HOBBES, LEVIATHAN, 89.

18. Powers, *Structural Aspects of the Impact of Law,* 1263.

19. *Id.* at 1291.

20. *Id.* at 1297.

21. *Id.* at 1265.

22. *Id.* at 1278.

23. HENRY DAVID THOREAU, WALDEN AND "CIVIL DISOBEDIENCE" 222–40 (New American Library 1960 [1949]).

24. RAWLS, A THEORY OF JUSTICE, 363–68.

25. Jules L. Coleman, *Efficiency, Utility, and Wealth Maximization,* 8 HOFSTRA L. REV. 521 (1979).

26. Herbert Simon, *Theories of Decision Making in Economics and Behavioral Science,* 49 AM. ECON. REV. 1–28 (1979); Richard Thaler, MISBEHAVING (W. W. Norton 2015).

27. HOBBES, LEVIATHAN.

28. LOCKE, SECOND TREATISE OF GOVERNMENT.

29. HOBBES, LEVIATHAN, 86–90.

30. THOMAS HOBBES, ON THE CITIZEN 12 (Richard Tuck & Michael Silverthorne eds. Cambridge Univ. Press 1997) ("Bellum omnium contra omnes").

31. LOCKE, SECOND TREATISE OF GOVERNMENT, 65–66.

32. ROUSSEAU, THE SOCIAL CONTRACT & DISCOURSES.

33. *Id.* at 3–4.

34. JEAN-JACQUES ROUSSEAU, JULIE, OR, THE NEW HELOISE: LETTERS OF TWO LOVERS WHO LIVE IN A SMALL TOWN AT THE FOOT OF THE ALPS 5–22 (Roger D. Masters & Christopher Kelly eds., Phillip Stewart & Jean Vache trans., Dartmouth College 1997 [1761]).

35. ROUSSEAU, EMILE, OR EDUCATION.

36. LOCKE, SECOND TREATISE OF GOVERNMENT, 46–47.

37. ROUSSEAU, THE SOCIAL CONTRACT, 19.

38. *Id.*

39. *Id.* at 15.

40. *Id.* at 35–36.

41. *Id.* at 54–56.

42. *Id.* at 55.

43. *Id.* at 63.

44. *Id.* at 13–14.

45. HOMER, THE ODYSSEY OF HOMER 189–90 (Richard Lattimore trans., Harper & Row 1965).

46. ROUSSEAU, THE SOCIAL CONTRACT at 18.

47. LENIN, THE STATE AND REVOLUTION.

48. BERTRAND RUSSELL, HISTORY OF WESTERN PHILOSOPHY 678 (George Allen & Unwin 1946).

49. IMMANUEL KANT, CRITIQUE OF PURE REASON 110–11 (Paul Guyer & Allan W. Wood eds. & trans., Cambridge Univ. Press 1998).

50. IMMANUEL KANT, GROUNDWORK OF THE METAPHYSICS OF MORALS (H. J. Paton trans., Harper & Row 1964).

51. IMMANUEL KANT, THE METAPHYSICAL ELEMENTS OF JUSTICE (John Ladd trans., Bobbs-Merrill 1965).

52. KANT, GROUNDWORK OF THE METAPHYSICS OF MORALS, 98–99.

53. *Id.* at 100.

54. *Id.* at 102.

55. *Id.* at 114.

56. *Id.* at 80.

57. *Id.* at 115–16.

58. *Id.* at 96.

59. KANT, METAPHYSICAL ELEMENTS OF JUSTICE, 35.

60. KANT, GROUNDWORK OF THE METAPHYSICS OF MORALS, 100–01.

61. KANT, METAPHYSICAL ELEMENTS OF JUSTICE, 43–44.

62. *Id.* at 35.

63. KANT, GROUNDWORK OF THE METAPHYSICS OF MORALS, 88.

64. *Id.* at 91.

65. *Id.*

66. *See, e.g.*, ONORA NELL (O'NEILL), ACTING ON PRINCIPLE: AN ESSAY ON KANTIAN ETHICS (Columbia Univ. Press 1975); BRUCE AUNE, KANT'S THEORY OF MORALS (Princeton Univ. Press 1979); MARCIA BARON, KANTIAN ETHICS ALMOST WITHOUT APOLOGY (Cornell Univ. Press 1995); CHRISTINE KORSGAARD, CREATING THE KINGDOM OF ENDS (Cambridge Univ. Press 1996).

67. KANT, METAPHYSICAL ELEMENTS OF JUSTICE, 76.

68. *Id.* at 78–80.

69. RAWLS, A THEORY OF JUSTICE.

70. *Id.* at 48–50.

71. *Id.* at 17–22.

72. *Id.* at 137.

73. *Id.* at 12.

74. *Id.* at 150–61.

75. *Id.* at 60–61.

76. *Id.* at 42–43.

77. *Id.* at 83–90.

78. *Id.* at 75–80.

79. *Id.* at 61.

80. *Id.*

81. *Id.* at 113.

82. *Id.* at 115–16.

83. Peter Westen, *The Empty Idea of Equality*, 95 HARV. L. REV. 537, 537–96 (1982).

84. RAWLS, A THEORY OF JUSTICE, 152–56.

CHAPTER 8: HISTORICAL SCHOOLS OF THOUGHT

1. The term derives from "Hermes," the name of the Greek messenger god.

2. Duncan Kennedy, *Form and Substance.*

3. J. M. Balkin, *Deconstructive Practice and Legal Theory*, 96 YALE L.J. 743 (1987).

4. *Id.* at 767; *see also* PATRICK ATIYAH, PROMISES, MORALS, AND LAW (Clarendon 1981).

5. PLATO, THEAETETUS, 152c6–8.

6. WILLIAM BLAKE, THE COMPLETE POEMS 128 (Alicia Ostriker ed., Penguin 1978).

7. THOMAS S. KUHN, THE STRUCTURE OF SCIENTIFIC REVOLUTIONS (Chicago Univ. Press 2nd ed. 1970).

8. FYODOR DOSTOYEVSKY, THE BROTHERS KARAMAZOV 297–316 (Andrew McAndrew trans., Bantam 1970).

9. CLAUDE LEVI-STRAUSS, STRUCTURAL ANTHROPOLOGY (Claire Jacobson & Brooke Grundfest Schoepf trans., Basic Books 1963).

CHAPTER 9: METHODOLOGICAL POLYTHEISM

1. J. R. R. TOLKIEN, LORD OF THE RINGS (Houghton Mifflin 1987).

2. HUBERT DREYFUS & SEAN KELLY, ALL THINGS SHINING: READING THE WESTERN CLASSICS TO FIND MEANING IN A SECULAR AGE (Free Press 2011).

3. Gerard Manley Hopkins, *Pied Beauty,* 1 THE NORTON ANTHOLOGY OF MODERN & CONTEMPORARY POETRY 78 (Jahan Ramazani, Robert O'Clair & Richard Ellman eds., W. W. Norton 3rd ed. 2003).

4. PHILIP BOBBITT, CONSTITUTIONAL FATE: THEORY OF THE CONSTITUTION (Oxford Univ. Press 1982).

5. Bobbitt uses the term "textual" to denote the first mode.—Ed.

6. Erie Railroad Co. v. Tomkins 304 U.S. 64 (1938).

7. Norway Plains Co. v. Bos. & Me. R.R. 67 Mass. 263 (1854).

8. Berenson v. Nirenstein 326 Mass. 285, 93 N.E. 2d 610 (1950).

9. W. B. Yeats, *The Second Coming,* 1 THE NORTON ANTHOLOGY OF MODERN & CONTEMPORARY POETRY 111 (Jahan Ramazani, Robert O'Clair & Richard Ellman eds., W. W. Norton 3rd ed. 2003).

10. Ghassemieh v. Schafer 52 M.D. App 31 (1982) (Md. Ct. Spec. App. 1982).

11. *Id.* at 38. *See* Garratt v. Dailey 279 P.2d 1091 (Wash. 1955).

Index